StratPro

**THE STRATEGIC
BUSINESS TRANSFORMATION
PROCESS**

StratPro

ALLEN E. FISHMAN

StratPro™: The Strategic Business Transformation Process

Published by Direct Communication Service, Inc.

Copyright © 2016 by Allen E. Fishman

Direct Communication Service, Inc

11031 Sheridan Blvd.

Westminster, Colorado USA 80020

Printed in the United States of America.

2016 – First Edition

Interior layout and design by: AuthorSupport.com

ACKNOWLEDGEMENTS

A special thanks to Dave Scarola and Dana Besbris for their review, input and editing on the book content. Thanks to Jodie Shaw for her work on the book cover and other design elements. I also want to provide a special thanks to Linda Anderson for her careful review of the book manuscript.

CONTENTS

INTRODUCTION

You don't have to stay in the rut of running your business based on the tyranny of the urgent. *StratPro®* will have you leading your business strategically so your organization can address the things that need timely action.

StratPro strategic business planning will impact every single component of your business, including how you make important business decisions and how every aspect of every job is accomplished. Using the StratPro strategic business planning process creates timely strategic change and decisions that will power your organization's journey to greater success.

The Strategic Business Transformation Process, which we call StratPro, is an easy-to-use strategic planning system that I started developing in 1980. The process was a major factor in the company I co-owned becoming so successful that it became a publicly owned company. The StratPro strategic planning process has benefited many types of organizations, from privately owned companies, to publicly owned companies, subsidiaries and divisions of publicly owned companies, government divisions, and even non-profit organizations. It is a tested and proven leadership process that has helped business leaders around the world, for decades, achieve greater profits and increase the value of their organizations.

StratPro encompasses everything you need to know for starting and implementing your organization's strategic planning, thereby achieving the desired results. StratPro is not a coaching process. Rather, it is a unique, holistic approach for strategically leading an organization to greater success. Although employees at any level in an organization will benefit from understanding StratPro, this book is directed to those in top management who are responsible for leading their organizations.

By using the StratPro strategic planning process, you will be taking the single most important step to reaching your organization's full potential. If your organization is already successful, StratPro will help your organization achieve greater success. If your organization is experiencing a lack of satisfactory results, StratPro will give you the insights and methods you need to lead your organization to achieve its full potential.

Reduces Ineffective Use of Time

StratPro can be adapted to the management time availability "bandwidth" of any organization, regardless of its size. When you first start StratPro, there is some diversion of top management time from working on day-to-day responsibilities to focus on strategic planning. But, it doesn't take long for StratPro to improve the effectiveness of time utilization, because it enables your management and non-management employees to focus on activities aligned with the goals of the organization. StratPro results in substantially reducing employee time and effort in areas that are not critical to the success of your organization. The result is that StratPro will create — rather than absorb — management and non-management time by creating new efficiencies and greatly reducing wasted time by all levels in your organization.

Gain Greater Commitment and Better Decision Making from Your Employees

By using StratPro, you will gain a collective commitment from your employees on organization critical success factors, goals, strategies and action plans. This will occur because your employees will share the same easy-to-understand picture of the strategic direction you wish to take your organization and the actions needed to get there.

The StratPro strategic planning process will help your managers make the right decisions in regard to resources, time allocation, and efforts for themselves and their subordinates. Lower-priority issues will be reduced, which will increase the accountability that comes from a disciplined follow-up mechanism in which action-plan results are reviewed against projected results and modified as needed to maximize outcomes.

StratPro Works For All Types and Sizes of Organizations

StratPro works effectively for all organizations, regardless of the type or size of the organization. When implementing StratPro, it is easy to customize the StratPro system to work best for your type and size of organization. For example, a smaller organization is not likely to have the same amount of management time to devote to the StraPro process as an organization with large annual revenue. Because of time availability, the regularly scheduled StratPro meetings with the *Strategic Leadership Team* may need to take place only monthly in a small organization rather than the weekly meetings recommended with large organizations.

Book Terminology

There are some uses of terminology in this book that I need to explain.

I often refer to the organization or division key decision maker as the **KDM.** This person is the organization leader who has the authority to make the key decisions on behalf of the organization. For private businesses the KDM is usually the owner. For larger public businesses, the KDM is often a department head.

I use the term **Strategic Leadership Team** or **SLT** to collectively refer to the KDM and the group of top managers the KDM chooses to work with in implementing StratPro.

I use the term **Direct Report** or **DR** to refer to an individual who reports directly to the Key Decision Maker.

Please note that although I use the term **annual revenue (a predominately American term)** for the amount of sales generated in a year, I recognize that different terminology might be used in your country, such as "annual turnover."

When I refer to a **Large-size** organization, I am referring to organizations with more than ten million in annual revenue. When I refer to a **Mid-size organization,** I am referring to organizations with between one million and ten million in annual revenue. When I refer to a **Small-size organization,** I am referring to organizations with less than one million in annual revenue.

Written Statements

Each of your organization preplanning steps, such as your Organization Vision Statement, and your actual StratPro Organization Plans require written StratPro statements, consisting of a series of clear, articulated bullet points, with individual written StratPro Statements not exceeding one-hundred words.

Composite Organizations Used As Examples

I have used examples of organizations to illustrate points for how StratPro can be applied. These organizations are actually composites of different organizations that have used the StratPro system, rather than specific organizations. Because of my desire to keep confidentiality for the specific organizations referred to, the names of the actual organizations and organization leaders, and even their industries, have been changed.

Please add the following sub-section to the intro – just before sub-section "You Are Now Ready to Start the StratPro Journey".

StratPro Workshops

This book explains all the key elements of the StratPro program with case studies and examples provided throughout. The best way to implement StratPro is using a series of workshops. The standard StratPro implementation is done through a series of workshops involving the full SLT. The workshops are either two hours or four hours, depending on the agenda, and involve "homework" to be done between sessions to make the workshops themselves as productive as possible.

The first six sections of this book correspond to the first six StratPro workshops. Once these workshops are completed, the Strategic Leadership Team will transition into monthly Organization Plan Monitoring Meetings, discussed in Chapter 17. StratPro also involves an annual 1-to-2 day Organization Planning Retreat to review the progress of the year, current status, emerging threats and opportunities and to update the plan as necessary for the upcoming year.

The following graphic illustrates the StratPro workshop model:

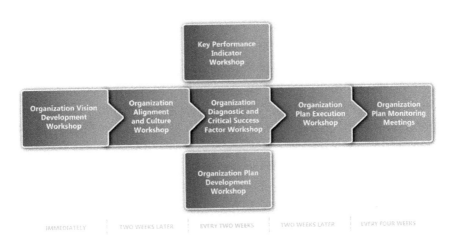

The key activities done in each workshop are shown in the following illustration. Note that each workshop activity is explained in detail in one of the Chapters within the Section corresponding to that workshop.

The workshops as best facilitated by a trained StratPro Implementer. However, some businesses may decide to implement it alone and this book provides the details for how to do this.

You Are Now Ready To Start the StratPro Journey

The collective parts of the StratPro system will have an amazing synergistic impact on your team's ability to develop strategic plans and use them to reach greater levels of success. But, for your organization to get the greatest amount of benefits from doing Strategic Planning using the tools and methods of StratPro, it requires a commitment to the entire process.

You and all the other members of your organization's SLT must ingrain the importance of StratPro strategic planning into your organization's culture. StratPro strategic planning must be totally embraced by you and your management team to get maximum benefit. Once StratPro strategic thinking is part of your organization management belief structure, "StratPro planning thinking" will trickle down through your entire organization, and "knee-jerk" reactions and "seat-of-the-pants" decisions will stop happening.

Your team members must both understand and follow the protocols required in the StratPro strategic planning process for StratPro to work most effectively for your organization.

As with any journey, there will be rough spots and your organization will need to make some unexpected detours. StratPro will empower you and your SLT to make the timely strategic changes that will power your organization's journey to achieving its optimal future.

Enjoy the journey!

SECTION 1

Organization Vision Development

In a strategically driven organization, the organization's vision statement is more than something put on the back of business cards or framed on organizations' walls. It brings clarity and focused purpose among the organization's employees. It serves as the foundation for your Strategic Leadership Team's strategic and, often, day-to-day decisions. A KDM should be able to use the Organization Vision to increase team building among the SLT, as well as teams of all levels within the organization.

The Organization Vision is meaningful whether the organization is a for-profit organization, nonprofit or government organization. With any type of organization, it provides the long-term framework needed to develop your organization's shorter-term plans, including the goal for each plan.

Effective strategic planning must start with clarity about the long-term vision of the organization, because it is a crucial tool to be used by the KDM and SLT to bring about greater success for the organization.

A clear and motivating organization vision helps to give purpose to employees. This, in turn, is one of the key factors in retaining quality employees for the long-term. Goals and even action plans involving individual employees or teams of employees need to be aligned with and leading to the achievement of the organization's vision of success.

An organization's vision gives a guideline for balancing priorities. It gives the direction for helping the SLT to determine the Key Performance Indicators that are used to track employee performance against well-defined objectives. It helps leaders determine where to allocate human resource budgets as to what positions are needed to have the greatest impact in achieving the organization's long-term vision.

In this book, you'll learn how to bring about "buy in" from employees at all levels to your organization's long-term vision. The vision statement will eliminate much of the dread of unknowns from economic down times and fuel plan growth during economic up times.

For those organizations that are privately owned, I've included a chapter in this section that shows the great impact of a business owner's personal vision statement on an organization's long-term vision statement.

CHAPTER 1

Organization Vision Statement

The objective of your Organization Strategic Plans is to empower your organization towards attaining your organization destination as identified in an organization vision statement. Therefore, the first priority is to identify that destination. This requires a written Organization Vision Statement.

In this chapter, you will learn the StratPro process for developing your written Organization Vision Statement. Only after your Organization Vision Statement has been identified and clarified in writing will your organization be able to create the most effective strategic plans to achieve this long-term vision.

So, before beginning your organization strategic planning, make sure there is a clear destination expressed in writing, one that is understood at all levels of the organization. Knowing the desired long-term destination for your organization will help your employees at all levels make day-in and day-out decisions and take actions that lead towards attaining the Organization Vision.

When you begin to develop your Organization Strategic Plans, which I will address later in this book, you will do so with knowledge that each factor in the Plans moves you towards reaching your Organization Vision. By doing so, you will avoid taking detours that deter your organization from reaching the desired destination. If there is not a clear Organization Vision, your management team will lead the organization on a course that may be seriously astray from reaching the long-term dreams for the organization.

There are many benefits of identifying the long-term destination of the organization beyond it serving as the destination for the organization strategic plans that you develop. Having a clear destination, which is realistically attainable, will create less stress, more happiness, and an overall harmonious alignment of the SLT's interaction.

By putting your vision for your organization's future in writing and sharing this future with your employees, your employees will be focused on a set destination. As noted business author Ken Blanchard stated "Leadership is the act of arousing, engaging and satisfying the motives of followers in an environment of ... change that results in the followers taking a course of action toward a mutually shared vision."

Your Organization Vision Statement will help you strategically lead your employees to the destination by inspiring commitment to the realization of your dream. With a clearly written Organization Vision Statement in place, you and your employees are more likely to pick the straightest path to your destination, including goals, strategies and action plans that will get you to your vision for the future of your organization.

What Exactly Is an Organization Vision Statement and What Does It Need To Contain?

Your SLT should clearly be involved in developing this desired destination. However, in a publicly owned company, the Board of Directors will often be deeply involved in determining the Organization Vision Statement. In a privately owned business, as will be further explained in Chapter 2, the business owner(s) will be involved.

The Organization Vision Statement is a picture of what the organization's desired success for five to ten years in the future looks like. Organization Vision Statements are long-term and usually don't need many changes for years at a time. These statements typically contain answers to certain questions I will now share with you.

The following questions will help you think about factors to consider for your Organization Vision Statement.

Principal Products and Services Factors

- What should your organization's principal products/services look like in five to ten years?
- What new products/services or business channels would you like to add?
- Which of your current products/services or business channels would you like to stop offering?
- What do you expect to be significantly different about your products/services or market approach in the future?
- What quality standards do you need to meet?

Operational Factors

- What operational activities do you want your organization to be outstanding in doing?
- What level of productivity and performance do you want from your organization?

Economic Factors

- What economic or financial results are integral to achieving your organization vision, such as operating on a sound financial basis or continuous profit growth?

Cultural and Values Factors[1]

- Why does your organization exist beyond what it provides for you and your family? (E.g. a desire to provide life-changing services to the business-owner community.)

---

1   More on these factors and how they impact on Team Alignment in Section 2 of this book

- What principles, beliefs and values are essential to your vision of the organization? (E.g. employee honesty and integrity that fosters an open, friendly and strategic workplace.)
- What social values, if any, would you like to see as part of the long-term vision of the organization? (E.g. contributing to a particular charity or cause or have a specific positive environmental impact)
- What is the desired management approach or philosophy?
- What is the philosophy for compensation and career growth opportunities for employees?

Customers and Clients Factors

- Who would you like as your future customers, clients or users?
- Do you have existing customers that you'd like to stop working with?

Headquarters Factors

- Do you want to relocate your organization's headquarters from your current location? If so, to where?
- Do you want the organization to own or lease its organization headquarters?
- Principal Outlets and Distribution Channels Factors
- In what geographical areas do you want to market your products/services?
- What current or other physical or virtual outlets/distribution channels would you like your organization to be using in the future?

Organization Position, Image or Recognition Factors

- What organization image do you seek in your industry, whether local, regional, national or international? (E.g. to be seen as the most innovative organization in your industry)
- What market share, if any, do you want for your organization? (E.g. 10% of all product sales for our products or being the

most successful locally, regionally, nationally or worldwide in your industry?)

100-Word Written Organization Vision Statements

As important as it is to identify all of the factors relevant to the Organization Vision, it is equally important to formulate the *most important factors* into a clearly defined and succinct written statement.

Your written Organization Vision Statement should not be viewed as a work of literary greatness. **Don't be too wordy!** It's difficult to include everything in the answers to the above questions, even if you think they are all important for the Organization Vision Statement. An Organization Vision Statement that is too wordy is likely to be misunderstood or ignored by employees.

The StratPro process forces you to prioritize and not be too wordy with the following guideline: your written Organization Vision Statement cannot exceed 100 words expressed in a series of clear and articulate bullet points or very short narrative statements. 100 words are all that is needed to create the desired organization long-term picture. Limiting your Organization Vision Statement to a 100-word written statement forces you to focus on key areas needed for that statement. All key factors should be very clearly and succinctly identified. The first draft of the Organization Vision Statement will probably be hundreds of words. The final version needs to cut the draft to no more than 100 words.

Below is an example of the Organization Vision Statement for Ride Away Company, which manufactures bicycles and sells and services other bicycle products:

- To be the city's largest provider of custom-made bicycles.
- To operate on a sound financial basis with steady profit growth.
- To be innovative without high risk.
- To have an open, friendly and strategic management approach to leadership.
- To retain highly productive, passionate employees who display honesty, integrity and teamwork.
- To have written processes and protocols for our staff.

- To have multiple outlets in high-traffic locations within fifty miles of our headquarters.
- To have a brand synonymous with high quality and service.
- To train our employees to provide outstanding services.

Example of Arden Construction Company's Vision Statement

- To provide commercial construction within three hundred miles of our headquarters.
- To be a leading provider of affordable, on-time, quality construction to our customers.
- To sell our services with honesty, knowledge and integrity.
- To use only high quality materials that can be bought at reasonable prices.
- To employ a loyal workforce that is passionate about the benefits of our services and motivated to help customers receive these benefits.
- To operate with a belief that there is more to business than profits.
- To work with like-minded subcontractors, clients and vendors.

Once the draft of your Organization Vision Statement is finished, review it from a standpoint of how it will be understood by your employees.

Communicating Your Organization Vision Statement

Once you, and all of the organization SLT members, know the desired organization destination, waste of your time and your employees' time and work efforts will be greatly reduced because you will have a clear direction. But, in order to achieve this, it must be pushed down to all levels of the organization.

If every one of your employees, not just the SLT, understands your Organization Vision and is working towards the same long-view dreams for the organization, all your employees, at all levels, will be making decisions that lead to achieving the Organization Vision. As a result, the vision is much more likely to succeed.

This communication can't be left to chance. The StratPro way requires that you take measures to ensure every employee connects their actions to helping achieve the long-term success of the organization. This focused effort won't happen if they don't understand the organization's desired destination.

Every decision at all levels within the organization should lead towards attaining your Organization Vision Statement — the dream for the organization's long-term future. Before finalizing your Organization Vision Statement, ask yourself if it will help your employees recognize what activities they need to focus on to help make the dreams for the future of the organization happen; and what activities they should stop doing because they are misaligned.

A good Organization Vision Statement keeps your employees engaged in a high level of challenge and stimulation while being grounded in reality. Excitement about the organization's vision can turn to lack of belief in organization leadership if you promote a vision that your employees believe to be unrealistic.

A realistic Organization Vision will help bring about a higher level of motivation. An unrealistic Organization Vision Statement results in demotivation and hurts the leadership team's credibility. Ideally, your Organization Vision Statement should create pride and motivation with your employees feeling they are part of something much bigger than themselves.

To maximize alignment within your organization, each of your employees needs to read and understand your Organization Vision Statement. Some organizations do this in a group setting, such as through Staff meetings. Others send it to their employees via email. Some organizations will periodically ask employees to repeat the essence of the Organization Vision Statement, providing a small reward if it is repeated correctly.

Sharing Your Organization Vision Statement Beyond Your Employees

Many organizations post their written Organization Vision Statements on their office walls, websites, and so on. The SLT from

Ride Away Company strategically displayed a condensed version of their Organization Vision Statement at the entrance of the company's premises, on their business cards and on their website for all to see.

Some organizations create an abstract of some expression(s) from their Organization Vision Statement as their organization Mission Statement, which they share on their websites. The construction company mentioned earlier has a Mission Statement formed into a tagline — "Affordable, On-Time, Quality Construction," is stitched into employee uniforms and appears in signage on company vehicles.

Writing an Organization Vision Statement

In creating an organization Vision Statement for a Public Company, a subsidiary or division of a publicly owned company or a nonprofit company, you don't need to consider the Personal Vision of any individual person or family, unless the person holds controlling voting rights. In using the StratPro system to bring about an Organization Vision Statement with publicly owned companies, subsidiaries or divisions of publicly owned companies or non-profits, the starting point differs.

If your company is privately owned, it is important you understand that the Organization Vision Statement must be in alignment with the personal long-term vision/desires of the business owner(s). This will be covered in the next chapter.

Each of the public companies with whom I have used the StratPro methods have had anywhere from hundreds of employees to thousands. These public companies have developed their Organization Vision Statement with input from the CEOs and other members of their SLTs, and sometimes the Board of Directors.

One public company that used the StratPro system had an eight-person SLT. Far and away the most dominant member of the team, for purposes of developing the Organization Vision Statement, was the CEO, who also had significant stock ownership in the company. When the draft of the Organization Vision Statement was completed by the SLT, it was shared with the board of directors. There were minor changes made, but the key factors stayed in place.

With respect to nonprofits, the starting point and the parameters for the written Organization Vision Statement are quite different. Each of the nonprofits I've worked with in developing a written Organization Vision Statement had clear charitable missions laid out in their organizational legal incorporation. The Organization Vision Statements had to satisfy, in every aspect, the company charter set forth of why they existed as a nonprofit.

One of the nonprofit companies was a school set up for a specific purpose. Another had stores where they sold donated clothing and merchandise. In each case, the executive directors of the nonprofits were the most influential in bringing about the key factors in the Organization Vision Statements, which were in line with the mission for which the nonprofits were created. Their SLT meetings were very free-thinking with ideas for the vision, but all involved had a clear understanding that everything in the written Organization Vision Statement had to be within the objectives stated for the nonprofits in their incorporation agreements.

Periodic Changes to the Organization Vision Statement

Your Organization Vision Statements should remain relatively constant unless a major change takes place in your organization or marketplace. However, your Organization Vision Statement is a living statement. Life "happens" and Organization Vision Statements will occasionally need a change. Set aside time periodically, at least annually, to review your Organization Vision Statement in light of changed circumstances

Events may take place that will require the rethinking and redefining of your Organization Vision Statement. Sometimes events occur that make your Organization Vision Statement no longer realistic.

There may be unexpected changes of circumstances that are so significant that your Organization Vision Statement needs to be reviewed right away. For example, marketplace change and new technology are among the most frequent causes of modifications to Organization Vision Statements. During an economic crisis that severely hurt the construction industry, Arden Construction's Organization Vision Statement was changed to eliminate language about operating within a three-hundred-mile region. This change took place during its annual "Turning the Wheels" retreat.

Another example of a change of circumstance was when Andrew Arden had two heart attacks in a short period of time. A revision of his Organization Vision Statement was needed to cut back on the level of desired expansion.

For some business owners, their views about family, charitable efforts, hobbies, or even spiritual pursuits may take on a greater importance in their life than their business, due to personal events that require them to revisit and modify their long-term dreams of organization success as expressed in the Organization Vision Statement.

Periodically review your Organization Vision Statement to make sure it is still meaningful to you and helps reinforce your focus on the desired destination. Consider changed circumstances that have occurred since you wrote your Organization Vision Statement. After considering these changes of circumstance, rethink what you want and what is realistic for your organization's long-term future.

Out of Sight–Out of Mind

Periodically, just reading your vision aloud in a group setting will help you stay focused on your desired destination. This periodic reading helps you and your employees avoid losing sight of your long-range target, which is easy to do with the multitude of day-to-day things fighting for your attention.

If and when you do decide to change your Organization Vision Statement, keep in mind that it may cause a ripple effect on your organization strategic plans that will need to be addressed.

Pre Planning

Your StratPro strategic planning is a journey with the destination being the achievement of your organization dreams. As with any journey, there are bound to be rough spots and even unexpected detours.

By nature, business leaders want to act right away. Too often, they start creating their strategic and action plans without standing back, taking in the landscape, and only then determining what the best strategic decision is in order to have the greatest chance of success. Certain essential preplanning must be completed before Strategic Planning is started. You need to start your StratPro strategic pre-planning efforts by first creating a written Organization Vision Statement.

CHAPTER 2

Alignment with Owner's Dreams for the Organization

If your organization is a privately owned business, you need to read this chapter. Because, in a privately owned business, the identification of what will be in the Organization Vision Statement is not handled in a democratic way. The Organization Vision Statement must be in alignment with the long-term dreams of the business owner(s). The business owner or owners need to be committed to achieving all the factors in the written Organization Vision Statement or the plans to achieve them will likely fail. If the business owner is not satisfied with any aspect of any Organization Plan, he/she won't support the Organization Vision Statement fully.

When the Organization Vision is in conflict with the business owner's dreams for the company, the business is not likely to attain the vision successfully. Consequently, the Organization Vision Statement must be in alignment with the business owner(s) dreams of what long-term company success looks like. If there is alignment, the business owners will be more likely to embrace their passion for the business.

SLT members, who are not the owners of the business, need to accept that the purpose of a privately owned business is to satisfy *the owner's* desires, not those of the employees.

Work/life balance, company image, recognition and family-member employee issues are often just as important, if not more important to the owner of a privately owned business than generating increased sales or profits. Sometimes this is very frustrating to other SLT members who have different ideas about what the best future of the business looks like. For instance, the personal vision of a business owner may not include maximizing profits. Instead it may include desires that involve employment for family members, or image in the community.

For example, Cooper Fabrication Company's Operations VP suggested, during a SLT meeting for creating an Organization Vision Statement, that the Cooper Fabrication Organization Vision Statement include regional offices, rather than the one office in which the company operated. The company CFO agreed with the Operations VP's recommendation and expressed that expanding into regional offices would result in the business owner, Carol, being able to take out hundreds of thousands of additional dollars a year in distribution income from the company.

To their surprise and frustration, Carol was not excited about expanding into regional offices. During the meeting, she explained that even though the expansion made great business sense, she was satisfied with the income she was already making and did not want to provide the additional personal commitment and involvement, such as out-of-town travel she felt would be required of her to make sure the expansion succeeded. Expansion into regional offices did not get included in the Organization Vision Statement.

Multiple Owners Bring Additional Challenges

To create an aligned Organization Vision Statement when multiple owners are involved, the owners need to resolve any areas of non-alignment they have about the future of the company before meeting with others on the SLT. The co-owners should be in agreement on key factors they want for the company five to ten years in the future and share these views with the SLT.

If key factors conflict with one another relating to the company's long-term future, these conflicts must be resolved before creating the Organization Vision Statement. A lack of alignment on the Organization Vision Statement by co-owners will negatively impact the effectiveness of the company's strategic plans. Managers will be rowing their oars in different directions. This is counterproductive to successful planning and implementation.

Expansion

One of the most common Organization Vision factors that co-owners may disagree on is how aggressively to expand the business, or whether to expand at all. Bat Vid Company had this happen when the co-owning brothers had conflicting views of expansion. Employees operated in conflict with each other because the company didn't have full owner support for the same strategic direction. Without alignment on the Organization Vision Statement, the two owners, at times, worked against each other, sometimes intentionally. Each harnessed the efforts of different managers to achieve a dream for the organization that was theirs alone. Some departments aligned with one owner and other departments aligned with the other owner.

Getting alignment by all the owners on the Organization Vision Statement may cause a delay in finalizing the statement, but it's worth taking the extra time. This requires compromise that does not give any of the co-owners exactly what they want but results in an Organization Vision Statement that meets the basic needs of all the co-owners for the long-term future of the organization. When co-owners create an Organization Vision Statement that is mutually acceptable, negotiations among the co-owners is typically necessary. This is best done with a professional facilitator who keeps the situation as unemotional as possible and focused on achieving mutually acceptable factors for the written Organization Vision Statement.

Co-Owners with Different Risk Willingness

At the time the first draft of the Organization Vision Statement was written for Parker Technologies, Phil and Paul, the brothers who co-owned the business, agreed they each wanted their company to expand to a minimum of three new major cities in the USA within the next ten years.

When this expansion factor in the draft was reviewed by the Parker's SLT, Parker's CFO explained that any banks willing to make the expansion loans would likely require Phil and Paul to personally guarantee the loans and new leases. Phil Parker responded that he was not willing to personally guarantee any additional company loans or new leases. After discussions, the brothers compromised with an agreement on an Organization Vision Statement with a less aggressive expansion: an expansion that could be handled out of company-generated cash flow without the brothers needing to co-sign new bank loans or guarantee new leases. The Organization Vision Statement agreed to operating offices in two additional cities.

Key Business Owner Factors to Consider when Crafting your Organization Vision Statement:

To clarify your long-term dreams for the future of your business, I've identified the following critical factors the business owner needs to consider. If there are co-owners, they need to be in alignment on the following:

- Desired income from company to support a certain level of material lifestyle
- Willingness to put personal assets at risk
- Personal passion to provide certain products or services
- Where your business headquarters will be located
- Where your products/services will be sold or your business will operate
- Family members employed in the business

Desired Material Lifestyle

For most business owners I have worked with on identifying their personal long-term visions of success, their desired material lifestyle is one of the first factors mentioned. Desired long-term compensation, distribution benefits and perks typically impact significantly on the destination owners want for their businesses. These factors affect such things as desired size of the company and the financial results of the business.

When I met with Andrew Arden, he expressed his desire to take out a specific annual minimum six-figure income from his company within five years. To do this, he recognized his company had to grow to a certain size to create income growth opportunities beyond this amount.

Willingness to Put Personal Assets at Risk

If the desire to eliminate personal guarantees is an important thing for an owner, it often affects the expansion potential and aggressiveness of a privately owned business. This impacts the Organization Vision Statement.

Desired Number of Employees

Some business owners want to have a certain number of employees. One client saw having over one-hundred employees as part of his dream because he defined this as owning a "big company." Andrew Arden, on the other hand, enjoyed very hands-on type work with his contractor company, Arden Construction. He didn't want to manage any more employees beyond the sixty he already employed. He wanted to grow, instead, by using subcontractors.

Business Headquarters Location

There is no right or wrong answer for where a business owner wants to live and work; there is only what is right for the business owner. The business should be located where the business owner desires.

Where Your Products/Services Will be Sold or You Will Operate

Many business owners want to limit where they sell their products/ services to areas in or around where they live. Often this is because of a desire to spend time with family. Carol Cooper, for example, expressed her desire to maximize time spent with her family. She decided against any additional out-of-town regional sales office expansion in her Organization Vision Statement because she wanted to decrease the amount of business travel required.

At Tipton, my partner and I wanted Tipton to have locations throughout the Midwest and Mid-south. When I formed TAB Boards International, my vision was for TAB to operate worldwide.

Family Members Employed In Business

A desire to employ family members in the business and even for them to have specific roles in the business are important factors for many business owners and should affect the Organization Vision Statement. If your Organization Vision Statement includes your business staying or becoming a family business, that desire is something you may want to share with your employees by mentioning this in your Organization Vision Statement.

Employing family members presents special challenges. If your business employs family members, or if you are considering doing so, I recommend that you read my book, *9 Elements of Family Business Success* (2009) published by McGraw Hill.

Once all owners have created a draft of the statement, it is time to get input from the rest of the SLT. It is important, however, that your SLT has the opportunity to express their views about the Organization Vision Statement before your company's written Organization Vision Statement is finalized. Their views often challenge key points in the first draft of the Statement because non-ownership members of the SLT often have a different perspective of what is possible. The SLT members often provide suggestions for better ways to express the Statement to make it more motivating without changing its essence.

SECTION 2

Organization Alignment and Culture

Creating the right role and culture fit for organization efficiency involves two key personnel-related factors. One is getting your people, particularly your managers, in roles that are good fits for them. This involves eliminating square-peg-in-round-hole situations. The second factor relates to creating the aligned organization culture needed to operate at peak efficiency.

CHAPTER 3

Role Alignment Factor

To maximize positive impact from your key employees, there must be alignment between what they do in your organization and what they should be doing. If the work roles fit between your key employees and the roles assigned to them, they will do a much better job of **PAVE**ing the road ahead, which will make your organization's ride to the destination of the written vision statement much easier. By having your key employees in the right roles, you will create a powerful engine that will propel your organization to greater success.

To Create Your Aligned Role You Need To Know Who You Are

In Plato's *Apology,* written nearly twenty-four centuries ago, Socrates says, "The unexamined life is not worth living." That sounds extreme, but it is certainly true that life must be examined carefully and reflected upon by those who expect true happiness and success. That definitely includes an organization's **Key Decision Maker (KDM)** and DRs. The secret here is for you to try to create as little or no gap between who you are and the work you do. To do this, you first need to know who you are. You should have a basic understanding and acceptance of who you are as a person. In this chapter, you will learn to look in the mirror, as you never have before, and conduct the kind of self-examination that will help you create Aligned Role fits.

Roles Outgrowing The Person

Finding role non-alignment is particularly common with organizations that brought on management when they were much smaller, but have kept them in the same roles as the organization has grown. This reality applies to business owners and anyone else in a managerial position.

When Armando, who has only a high school education, started his restaurant and catering business, it was just one small restaurant. Several years later, its annual revenue was over five-million dollars. As his business grew, he realized he needed to stay out of certain areas, such as accounting or operational matters, and instead focus on areas that took advantage of his passion for interacting with people. He has a knack for making people want to do business with him. It is amazing how people gravitate to him. Armando recognized and used those strengths to create a role for himself that has had a lot to do with the outstanding success of his business. This type of role alignment of the business owner has been a key element behind the success of many privately owned businesses.

When one parts-distribution company was very small, the best salesperson in the company was promoted to sales manager. The company grew from doing several hundreds of thousands per year in revenue to doing tens of millions of dollars per year. In going through the role alignment part of the company's first StratPro strategic planning process, it was clear the sales manager was not truly a manager. He was capable of doing many things of value to the company but didn't have some of the natural leadership characteristics necessary to be effective in managing what had developed into a much larger organization. He didn't enjoy managing people and was not a motivator by nature. He was highly compliant and great with follow-through on anything asked of him. The result was a realignment of his responsibilities so that he was focused on operations, a role that fit better. He was very effective in operations because it fit who he is. Someone else was given the sales manager role. This person was very effective and his motivational techniques made a major positive impact on company results.

In another company that has less than ten employees, a man with the greatest amount of operations knowledge in the company became the Director of Operations. As the company grew, almost everyone who worked with him knew he was in the wrong position, but nothing was done about it. His basic behavioral style made detail and process type work stressful, whereas interacting with people fit his personality. The KDM, however, kept him as Director of Operations regardless of how many people gave him information about the man doing a poor job running his department. A change did not take place until the company went through the role-fit diagnostic that is part of the StratPro strategic planning process. One of the results of the process was moving the Director of Operations to Director of Customer Relations — a position that better matched his natural love of interacting with people.

PAVE

Role alignment is needed so that key employees are doing roles that best fit them. This results in your key employees being able to PAVE their way to being higher-impact employees. This leads to greater organization results. The acronym PAVE represents four important criteria for identifying an employee's true competitive-edge strengths.

P: Do you have a strong **Passion** for doing this?

A: Do you have a strong **Aptitude** for doing this?

V: Does this support the "big picture" **Vision** of the long-range future of the organization, as expressed in your Organization Vision Statement?

E: Can you do this while maintaining an **Empathetic** Personality?

Determine the current level of "fit" by assessing whether a person's current position best matches his/her **P**assion, **A**ptitude and Vision

> *High Impact business leaders understand and accept who they are. The starting point is honest self-assessment.*

of where he/she wants to go next in their lives. Then examine whether the roles have an Empathetic Behavioral/Personality Match with his/her basic nature.

P – Look First for Passion

We'll start with 'P', which stands for the first (and probably easiest to remember) element, Passion. Many years ago, my father told me, "People who dread going to work usually fail. So, whatever you decide to do, select something that makes you excited to get up and go to work." Over the years, I have found you can have all the ability in the world but still be unable to be a high-impact manager or owner, if you don't feel positive passion for what you do at work. Doing that for which you feel passion is a major factor that separates high-impact managers and successful business owners from those who perform at low-impact levels. We are more likely to excel at doing the things we enjoy and look forward to doing.

Passion is a key element in the formula for success adopted by most high-impact managers and business owners. When you have passion for what you are doing, you may wake up in the middle of the night with new ideas and solutions to problems. You are motivated to do these things because you love what you do — not because you have to do it. Passion for doing your role can become an obsession; but you won't suffer from burnout because you are enjoying what you do. Many individuals who have gone through the role-alignment exercises of StratPro have mentioned how they often had to stop themselves from spending so much time thinking about how to make things better in areas they enjoyed.

When we have passion in the workplace, we feel vibrantly alive and engaged. Without passion, your SLT members are more likely to be among those who are shuffling mindlessly through work—merely going through the motions.

Sure, we all have to perform work tasks we'd love to delegate, but what if the stuff you hate to do was all or most of what you are supposed to be doing.

Those whose roles involve activities for which they have no passion are unlikely to be high-impact performers because they will not give maximum effort to achieve results.

You can have outstanding aptitude for something. But, if you are not consistently giving it your all, it is likely you have no passion for it. At best, managers will be bored, unhappy and only going through the motions when doing activities for which they have no passion. At worst, they will have a level of depression and be unsuccessful.

> *If there's no joy most of the time in one's work, we will not be inspired to do our best work.*

It's not unusual to find business owners and key executives who dread going to work because they have no passion for their job roles. You will also find increasing stress in your work responsibilities if most of your work involves doing things for which you feel no passion. One VP of a company said that performing some of the functions of his job "often feels like torture." In contrast, I have never met someone who suffered from burnout as the result of doing things that are his/her true passions.

You might have the ability to excel in specific business-related activities, but you will be unlikely to give it your best effort in the long run without a driving passion for doing those activities. This driving Passion creates great focus and ensures you end up with results that simply cannot happen without that level of focus.

Driving passion is what gets things done at a high level of excellence. Every great piece of work you have ever been truly inspired by was almost certainly the result of a driving passion: the Sistine Chapel, Disneyland, Facebook, you name it. As a result, identifying the business areas for which you have a true and driving passion is the first and, perhaps, most important step when it comes to Role Alignment.

To illustrate this first part of the PAVE self-examination process, let me share some examples of my own driving passions in the workplace. I feel passion for creating processes with protocols that help our facilitator/coaches deliver greater value to our customers. Often, I get ideas that pull me away from whatever I am doing. I spend much of my typical day focused on creating or refining these processes — thank goodness! My driving passion for these activities urges me to focus on them relentlessly and with great enthusiasm.

If you feel passion for something you do at work, it's likely the work-related activities you are engaged in when you feel that passion are suited to your natural personality/behavioral style. The classic clue: You don't have to adapt or force yourself to do these activities. No one has to "motivate" you to undertake these activities.

On the other hand, if the required activity is contrary to your natural personality/behavioral style, you will undoubtedly feel stress. It's likely you can identify these activities fairly easily, too.

The bottom line is this: If the business activities you choose are in strong enough harmony with your basic personality/behavioral style to elicit passion, you will enjoy the experience. If they aren't, you won't.

During one of our first strategic planning sessions, Bridget, who owns an ergonomic office furniture manufacturing business, identified the activities for which she has driving passion. These activities involved interacting and doing business development with key client prospects. She pointed out the large amount of sales her activities in this area generated for her company. Bridget, as it turns out, is strongly socially driven and loves using her ample selling skills to open new major accounts. These activities greatly benefit the company.

After recognizing these factors, she made changes resulting in delegating over 50% of her time on administrative type matters so that she could focus on creating, developing and maintaining strong relationships with key-account customers.

Employees who have learned how to spend most of their time doing the things they love demonstrate passion to burn at work. These people generally don't mind taking on a few unpleasant tasks along the way, because, overall, they love what they do. These are the kinds of people that make it easy for KDMs to inspire and lead.

A – Aptitude

It is a very rare individual, indeed, who is outstanding in all areas of business. The vast majority of business leaders go into the game with identifiable aptitude strengths and weaknesses. There are some things we're just plain better at compared to others.

When identifying your aptitude strengths, look for your strongest aptitudes. For most of us, it is fairly easy to identify the areas in which we excel. These are the areas in which we have a competitive edge. If you do not have strong aptitude in a particular business activity, it almost goes without saying that you won't excel in it over the long term, no matter how passionately you may feel about the activity. You can love doing something but never be good at it. So having driving passion without aptitude is not going to be enough to put an activity among your Personal Business Strengths.

Sometimes, SLT members struggle to identify their premier abilities when asked to identify them during the strategic planning exercises. If you have trouble seeing your best abilities, ask those you work with, and even family or friends, what they think are your greatest strengths.

One Director of Human Resources for a company told me that there was no area in which she was outstanding. When speaking to her fellow SLT members about her, they expressed a much brighter picture of her aptitudes. One of the members told me she had remarkable people skills and that she was a natural leader who easily got her employees to do what she wanted. Another pointed out that she brought great value as a company team member due to her insights and advice. He said she helped create a great company work culture and was outstanding at getting the most out of employees.

> *Regardless of how great you may be at something, if you don't enjoy doing it, you will not put your heart into it and the results will not be your best.*

The Operations VP of one company listed an aptitude for creating systems, protocols and processes. If you asked ten people who have worked with her on whether she is better at creating systems and processes than the average person, I believe at least nine out of ten of those people would instantly say yes. I offer this example to give you a clear sense of what an aptitude is (and isn't). If you asked those same ten people about her aptitude to manage salespeople, a very different consensus would emerge!

Multiple Aptitudes/Strengths

Most of us have numerous areas in which we have strong aptitudes. Start by writing down those activities on which you spend a lot of your business time right now that involve one of your aptitude strengths.

Example of Aptitude Fit

Jeff has great ability/aptitude for gaining new clients with different marketing methods. In his case, his role as VP of Marketing certainly leads to the company attaining its long-term vision of success.

V – Vision for Big Picture Potential

High Impact business leaders spend more of their time on Big Picture Potential activities than on activities that do not have the potential to help the big picture of the organization. Each SLT member should ask themselves: "What can I do that has the potential to make a major positive impact on the organization?" We are talking here about activities that bring the organization closer to achieving the Organization Vision Statement discussed in Section 1 of this book. Recall that Bridget's "Big Picture Potential" activities to close sales and create new relationships fell into this category.

Just because you are passionate about doing certain things, and better than the average person at doing them, does not mean that any of those things should be major workplace time investments.

The smaller your organization, the more likely it is that you may have to spend a lot of your time doing things you don't enjoy, may not have great aptitude for and that may not have Big Picture Potential. In small organizations, you just have to make sure they get done to a certain level of competence because there is no one else to do these things.

Activities that have low Big Picture Potential are among the first to be delegated when an organization grows and can put on more infrastructure. The question is whether and how you can transition your efforts to focusing less of your time on those activities.

One man told me that before he started his software organization, he had been a financial officer for another company. While in that position, he had enjoyed and been quite successful at mergers and acquisitions. He mentioned there was currently great opportunity for buying companies in his field, but that doing so would take a lot of time away from things he was responsible for that did not have Big Picture Potential.

I asked him to develop an outline that identified any work activities on which he spent more than twenty hours a month. It turned out he was spending twenty to thirty hours a month helping to prepare his company's financial statements — even though he had qualified accounting staff. He was spending many hours doing things he was good at that had no Big Picture Potential.

When we finished discussing his activities, he realized he should be using those twenty to thirty hours a month using his ability in mergers and acquisitions, which he was good at, enjoyed doing, and also had definite Big Picture Potential.

Each member of the SLT needs to identify "which areas of passion, for which I have outstanding aptitude, have the potential to help the organization gain the greatest results from my work activities." An organization leader should not be focusing most of his or her work time doing things that do not have Big Picture Potential, even if they have great Passion and Aptitude for doing those things.

E – Empathetic Behavioral/Personality Match

E, the last element of the PAVE acronym, tends to be the one that many people don't understand the first time they see the PAVE formula. By saying, "Empathetic behavioral/personality match," I mean "doing the type of work that matches your own natural style of behavior."

Within each of us is a set of characteristics — ways of thinking, feeling and acting — that mark our natural behavior or personality as individuals. Most of us should have a good understanding of what activities feel like a natural extension of who we are, rather than something forced and unnatural. It's important that each member of the SLT begin the process of understanding "who I am" and what activities make you feel as though you are identifying and empathizing with your own "natural self."

Sometimes we have to dig around a little, ask a few pointed questions and commit to some level of research in order to help us better understand what it is that makes up our natural behavioral style. One way to help identify the "natural you" is to use a personality or behavioral survey. There are many resources that can inexpensively provide an accurate analysis of your personality/behavioral style. Most of these take only ten to fifteen minutes of answering questions in survey form. One such system is the DISC survey, which I would strongly recommend your organization invest in for all SLT members.

There are many different resources that use the DISC model as the basis for their analysis. The surveys identify natural behavioral styles as they involve dominance, influence, steadiness and compliance. You can learn more about DISC at http://www.thediscpersonalitytest.com.

There is no right or wrong behavior nature. You just want to create a fit with your real nature. It is important to be honest with yourself about the natural you (the personality or behavior you were born with) versus the adapted you (the personality or behavior you assume or adapted to because of your environment).

Good Role/Behavioral Fit

Keith is the Director of Sales for an IT software company. The fit is good because he has a very high natural I (Influence) on the DISC scale, with passion for social interaction and a knack for making people want to do business with him. He genuinely loves networking. His sales staff enjoy working for him. Using his people skills is something Keith relishes, and the stellar sales record of his team proves he's good at it.

Keith's social skills also happen to be important in his sales management job. No one needs to be forcing Keith to get out and motivate his sales staff to sell and network. His desire to do so comes from a place of fit with his personal natural behavioral style.

Keith's role has an **Empathetic** personality match; there are no gaps between who Keith is and the work he does.

Bad Role/Behavioral Fit

Ideally you would want your head of sales to manage those who enjoy selling organization products/services. At the same time, it is very common that this type of person may dread or, at a minimum, not feel comfortable doing administrative work or developing operational protocols. Some SLT members have expressed that they "feel uncomfortable or funny" about doing such things as negotiating deals, handling employee conflict, firing employees and conducting employee reviews. In light of this, it should be clear their responsibilities should not require much involvement in these areas.

While working at an accounting firm during college, the partners recognized me for what they termed my "outstanding aptitude" for the work. They offered me an early partnership if I agreed to employment with the firm after graduation. It was an appealing offer, but the problem was that I hated doing accounting work. I was good at it, but I had no passion for the work. Every day that I went to work, I felt nothing but dread for what I was doing.

When Role Fit is Not Possible

There are times when you cannot solve a role-fit problem among your SLT members by revising the job description of the SLT member. In these situations, you need to do the right thing both for the organization and that SLT member. In one distributorship, a person without a high level of academic background in accounting was in charge of finances, among other things, when the organization was small. As the organization grew, his lack of aptitude in the area became an increasing problem.

The KDM tried to solve the problem by sending him to finance courses. But, it didn't solve the problem. The organization lost a very talented accounting staff member who reported to the Accounting Manager. He explained he was leaving because there was no way to move up, and he was far better in accounting and finance projects than the man he was reporting to.   There was a discussion between the KDM and a few of the SLT members on where this person could fit in the organization if he didn't head up accounting. The feeling was that there was no fit. Ultimately, after a lot of soul searching, the KDM had a very frank conversation with the man and set out a plan for him to exit over the next year. The organization paid for and engaged an outplacement firm to work with him to help him land a job with a smaller organization that required less sophistication in their accounting staff. At the same time, more of his responsibilities were turned over to his selected successor, and a development schedule was put in place for her.

Several months before the year was up, a position was found for the Accounting Manager, heading up accounting at an organization that had only one other person working in the accounting department.

No Right Or Wrong Natural Behavioral Style

Work activities either match or do not match a person's natural behavioral style. If there isn't a match between your natural behavioral style and most of the kind of things you're doing at work, you will be in conflict with your natural behavior rather than in empathetic match, which will create stress. Without knowing the natural you, you will be unable to reduce stress in your work by focusing your efforts on doing that which fits your natural behavior.

The greater the gap between your natural behavior and the behavior needed to do your job responsibly, the more stressed you will become. Bottom line — you need to do what you are suited for if you want to prevent work stress and burnout.

Each SLT member needs to know his or her natural personality or behavioral nature. Once you know your natural behavior style, it is time to share this information with fellow team members. This will allow the SLT members to look at the roles assigned to all the members, including the KDM, and to discuss how to best reallocate the responsibilities to create the best fit with behavior styles. Another benefit of sharing this information is that it will help each member understand the best way to communicate with other members based on their natural behavior style.

Now Fit The Right Peg With The Right Hole

The closer the role fit, the more likely each of your organization leaders will share one trait: an obsession channeled in a positive direction that requires great performance to be satisfied. The result of having great organization SLT role-fit alignment will be that your organization's managers become *exponentially* more motivated, efficient and productive in areas that directly affect the success of your organization.

So, take the necessary time to review the role-fit analysis carefully for each SLT member. Then consider revisions to the job descriptions of your organization leaders so that what they do better reflects their known or uncovered strengths, motivations and attitudes. The bottom line is: you need to "do what you are" in order to give your best efforts and deliver the strongest results to your organization.

High Impact Mangers Have High Competitive-Edge Strength Fit

If most of what you do meets all four of the PAVE criteria, you have what I refer to as a Competitive-Edge Strength Fit. If you focus seventy-five percent of the time you spend working in areas that use your Competitive-Edge Strength Fit, your positive impact on your organization will be much greater, and you will get more satisfaction from your business involvement.

High-impact managers typically spend at least seventy-five percent of their time in business activities that fit all their PAVE factors. In contrast, I believe that most underperforming managers spend less than twenty-five percent of their time on business activities involving activities that fit all four of their PAVE factors.

Your workday should be built mostly around doing what you love doing, you do well, and were born to do. It is the objective of the StratPro strategic planning process to ensure these types of activities become most of your daily reality. Engage assertively with your KDM to make sure this happens. But you can't do that unless you identify exactly WHAT IT IS that you love doing and can do well!

> A Competitive-Edge Strength Fit must meet all four of the PAVE criteria. Unless you love doing it, are great at it, can deploy it in such a way that it brings a "big bang" to your organization's success, and you know it creates no gaps between who you are and what you do, it's not a Competitive-Edge Strength Fit that deserves most of your work time.

Take some time now to examine what you do over the course of a single day at work, recurring over a week, month or calendar quarter. Place a star by all those tasks for which you feel passion. When you're done, you should identify a clear list of the things for which you *do not* feel passion. Once you do this, you'll have the first element that defines a Competitive-Edge Strength Fit. How do you delegate those functions you abhor so you can create a balance that eliminates negative factors that lead to undue stress and burnout?

The challenge now is to create a plan for how, over a period of time, you clear away the tasks that definitely don't inspire your passion. Now look at the remaining items to see if they fit the other three parts of the PAVE formula. Each member of the SLT should ask the following:

- Do I have strong aptitude for this activity for which I feel Passion?
- Does this activity have Big Picture Potential?
- Does the activity fit well with my natural behavior/personality?

For some, there is value in creating a written personal Competitive Edge Role Strength Fit Statement, of not more than one-hundred words, that matches desired activities with the results of the PAVE analysis. Writing down this information solidifies and secures your thoughts, will help you catch any inconsistencies and identify what you may need to learn about yourself.

The emphasis in this chapter has been on creating the best role fit with each member of the SLT, even the KDM. But, it cannot stop there. It starts with the top leaders because role fit is not likely to take place in lower echelons of the organization if top managers do not have role fit. But it is up to each member of the SLT to push down the same process in bringing about role fit to every level that ultimately reports to the manager.

Strategic Leadership Team Members' Fit for Being Team Members

SLT members should include only those who report directly to the KDM. The SLT should never include any employee who reports to any other member of the Team. Consider, for example, the potential conflict and disruption to your SLT if both your Vice President of Marketing and your Director of Marketing, who reports to your Vice President of marketing, were to be on your Management Team.

It is not necessary that all managers who report to the KDM be on the SLT if this is a large number of managers. Your management team should be limited to a small number, ideally not more than six organization executives who report directly to KDM plus, of course, the KDM. Other executives and managers will be invited to attend portions of SLT meetings, as needed, to share their views and provide feedback on specific issues.

The lynchpin for great interaction is that the person running the team meetings be exceptional at being a facilitator. Select only managers for inclusion in the SLT who will openly and honestly express their views. Don't make the mistake of choosing SLT members who are "rubber stamps" or "yes" people. Your organization results will suffer if the SLT members blindly agree with everything the KDM believes. Your Management Team must feel comfortable sharing different views among themselves and your organization KDM.

CHAPTER 4

Developing the Organization Culture Needed For Alignment

Creating and sustaining an effective, aligned organization culture is one of the fundamentals that will drive truly great results in every organization. In a business context, "organization culture" is the shared values and practices of organization employees. It is "how we do things around here." It is the unique way organization employees interact with each other and the world. Ideally, Organization Culture is the *practice* of clearly articulated organization values, such as meeting timeliness, honesty and commitment to deliver quality products or services.

Culture plays an important role in most successful organizations. Investing time and other resources to bring about cultural alignment provides a great return on investment because **a fully aligned organization culture propels organizations forward to greatness.** The flip side of this is that an unaligned culture typically holds organizations back from fulfilling their potential. I learned years ago to not be surprised that most underachieving organizations I came into contact with have unaligned cultures.

> *An aligned workplace culture is like a roof that protects your organization when rough weather rolls in.*

If you've ever felt a disconnect between the way someone in your organization *says what* behavior is supposed to be and the way it actually is, then you have personally experienced an unaligned, dysfunctional workplace culture. In a way, it can be viewed like a **hole in the roof of the cultural house**.

Organizations with a clear and aligned culture typically outperform competitors that lack such a culture by substantial margins. Some studies report the difference at 200% or more in key metrics! (Footnote: *http://management.about.com/cs/generalmanagement/a/companyculture.htm)*

Organization culture — "the way we do things around here"— is inevitably the result of certain VALUES that drive behavior. If our stated values match up with what we do and the decisions we make, we can say our workplace culture is in Alignment. Our stated values are also our behavioral values. Organization values will serve as the "compass point" by which decisions are made and disputes resolved within the organization.

Organization Culture Starts At The Top

The first draft of the words chosen for the Organization Culture Statement, which will be discussed in detail later in this chapter, are typically first brought up by the KDM as what he or she wants for the organization. The KDM should make his/her desires for the culture of the organization clear by communicating this culture and following up with actions that are in alignment with such culture.

> *How we actually do things must match up with what we say. Organization culture values must be reinforced and demonstrated by management's behavior if you want other employees to follow it.*

Then the Organization Culture Statement is reviewed

with the SLT, where feedback from all members of the SLT is given before it is finalized. Organization Culture reflects the values of the KDM but the final identified culture is usually greatly influenced by the organization's DRs.

The KDM, and all other members of your SLT, must agree, or at least act in a way that agrees, with your organization's unique culture, as communicated from the top. For you to have your desired aligned organization culture, you must support and embrace the culture with your actions on a daily basis. You will either be supporting or undermining the stated culture of your organization with the way you address your work practices, decision making and all your interactions with other employees at all levels, day to day.

> *When your Organization Culture Statement is posted on the wall and there are no role models in top management to follow, a list of stated values could do more harm than good!*

Identifying the desired productive workplace culture and bringing out the desired culture of an organization is primarily the responsibility of the SLT. Organization SLTs are the most important influence in shaping the organization culture. Organization culture is reflected in what we do, not what we say. What we do includes the standards of behavior we, starting with the KDM and proceeding through all the DRs, personally do and the actions we accept from others.

The process of bringing about cultural alignment can be done quickly, smoothly and without a lot of stress for the organization if the KDM and the DRs all live by and "walk the walk" of the desired culture. In most organizations, it is actually the DRs who have the greatest impact on bringing about the desired aligned organization culture because they are in the greatest amount of contact with the organization employees.

Just as there are functional and dysfunctional families, there are functional and dysfunctional SLTs. Think of the last time you went to a supermarket on a very busy shopping day. Doubtless, you saw many families in the aisles. Some of those parents and kids interacted harmoniously and made decisions about where to go next and what to buy, with little evident conflict or hard feelings. Other groups fought loudly and openly, spoke inappropriately, or even had major public meltdowns (and I'm not just talking about the toddlers). The difference: some families have established a functional system of values — also known as a *culture* — that supports both their relationships and their decision making. For other families, it's evident the system is still, shall we say, a work in progress. It's exactly the same with teams and organizations.

If you expect to develop an effective, aligned organization culture, recognize that talk alone doesn't do it. You can spend all day and night talking to your employees about your expectations concerning organization culture, but nothing is likely to take place without action from the KDM and the DRs. In the final analysis, the organization's everyday working culture is based primarily on what the KDM and the DRs *do*—and not on what they *say* the culture should be.

The single most important relationship when it comes to strengthening or weakening alignment with the desired organization culture is the relationship between the KDM and the DRs. The way your KDM talks to members of the SLT will send signals to the whole organization about what is and isn't an acceptable and expected way to communicate. It will also communicate what is and isn't permissible in terms of one-on-one communication with employees. That means each KDM has a personal and organizational obligation to make the right cultural choices — on a daily basis — in his/her interactions with the DRs. However, it does not stop with the KDM doing the right things for the culture when interacting with DRs.

Inaction will also shape culture. If what members of the SLT say doesn't match up with what's done by any of them, there's a hole in the roof of the organization's cultural house. Negative organization culture forms if members of the SLT ignore and don't penalize bad behavior. The organization earns the culture it creates. Employees adopt certain cultural behaviors based on their experiences. A lack of rewards for behavior consistent with the desired culture will communicate to employees that the behavior is not important. If KDMs and DRs don't reward positive behavior, subgroups that will not support unrewarded organization culture objectives will form.

According to Professors Ken Thompson (DePaul University) and Fred Luthans (University of Nebraska), we learn to rely on certain workplace behaviors based on the positive or negative consequences of those behaviors. If a certain behavior is rewarded, we tend to repeat it, and the repetition makes it more likely to be accepted as part of our daily working culture. The same is true in reverse — if a behavior is connected with punishment, or any intense negative emotion, we are less likely to repeat it.

To achieve remarkable positive results for your organization, the SLT has an important role to play in bringing about true cultural alignment — the kind of alignment that goes beyond "lip service."

Every member of the SLT affects the culture; whether the manager likes it or not. Something seemingly simple, like receiving a heartfelt "thank you" from a manager when a job is completed with a high degree of competency, can carry immense cultural implications. The clothes worn at the office by the SLT, for example, send powerful signals to the rest of the organization about how formal the workplace is or isn't. If a member of the SLT responds abusively to mistakes or feedback with which they don't agree, that inevitably affects the workplace culture in a negative way. If SLT members

> *It is up to the SLT to identify, embody and reinforce the right workplace culture. Cultural alignment will not happen overnight, but if you work together in good faith, it will happen.*

are quick to congratulate the team for good work, this action inevitably shapes the culture in a positive way. And if your organization KDM or any DR keeps erratic work hours, and is gone from the business for long periods of time, that sends the rest of the organization important signals about the expected work ethic.

How Do You Change A Dysfunctional Culture?

Eliminating a dysfunctional organization culture does not come about by accident. Very often, I have heard comments from SLT members complaining about such things as, "we have said over and over to our people that they have to do more hours prospecting", or "they need to learn more about technology" or whatever it is they say needs to change. But the problem is the culture. They talk about how they repeat over and over how the culture needs to change, but it doesn't happen. I have to hold my smile back when I hear this. Culture doesn't change by talking; it changes from actions. Whether the actions are rewards or punishments, talk alone is ineffective.

Eliminating dysfunctional culture and bringing about an aligned culture that gives your organization a competitive advantage starts with all your organization SLT members being committed to what is needed to bring about the desired workplace culture. Each culture challenge is different, and you may need a different strategy for correcting the problem.

If dysfunctional cultural behaviors are left unaddressed, this likely will damage your efforts to have an aligned culture. What really matters is how you respond when it happens. Regardless as to whether the cause of the problem is action or inaction, you need to address this situation with **tactful, persistent engagement to keep the desired culture of the organization in alignment.**

Most organization employees *already know, intuitively,* what a productive workplace culture *is* and how it functions, and what cultural dysfunction looks like. If you're exploring a situation where an employee has violated the organization culture, try to find out if the employee realizes that he/she has violated the required organization culture. It's also imperative that you have the discussion in a one-on-one setting with the employee and that you focus on the behavior, not the person. Your challenge is different if you're dealing with a group culture problem.

When sitting in the hot tub one day in Hawaii, I met a man who worked for an organization from the mainland that had bought out a company in Hawaii. The parent organization transferred him from the mainland to Hawaii to help integrate the culture of the acquired company with that of the parent organization. He was explaining that the Hawaiian company had been a family business. Soon after starting his assignment, he recognized the culture allowed for a large number of employees, many of whom had worked for the company for decades, to bicker with each other. In addition, their dysfunctional culture included a lack of acceptance of responsibility. The initial strategy of pointing out that this culture was insufficient did not change things.

The solution came about from an action plan that included calling daily meetings focused on accepting responsibility and how to properly interact with each other. At the beginning of the meeting, the man read the following to the employees:

- Employees must keep their word, be truthful, not mislead anyone and not misrepresent anything.
- We will succeed as a team. This success requires direct communication that embraces respect and is without hidden political agendas. Your career path will be limited and the future financial viability of the organization will be in question if we do not eliminate the internal politics common in the organization.
- When an employee is wrong, the employee is expected to acknowledge that he or she is wrong, rather than make excuses.
- Employees must keep all internal communications confidential.
- Employees must recognize the importance of and fully support organization systems, processes, procedures and protocols.
- T.E.A.M. (Trust, Engagement, Acceptance, and Measurement)

Another example involved Bob, a KDM in a manufacturing company, who told me that a culture had evolved in his company that he described as an I-never-make-mistakes attitude. This, he felt, was a factor in the company consistently falling well short of Bob's goals for the organization. Bob decided to eliminate the I-never-make-mistakes attitude by creating a written Organization Culture Statement that included a sentence that employees were expected to admit their mistakes and not make excuses.

Bob then evangelized and reinforced this culture through his own direct actions with his DRs. He made it clear with words in the Organization Culture Statement, and with his actions, that if you make a mistake, own up to it! It took a while, but the company eventually moved beyond the I-never-make-mistakes attitude. This one critical point in the Organization Culture Statement helped to transform his company and dramatically improved its performance.

Aligning an unaligned culture is literally impossible. All DRs are responsible for embodying and acting in accordance with a positive workplace culture, so that they serve as a cultural role model for the entire organization.

Special treatment also causes cultural alignment problems. There will be times when you may find yourself with an employee who, if allowed to, will try to be treated "special." Jan, a business owner, developed with the help of all her eight DRs, a written Organization Culture Statement that included a clear reference to "on-time arrival for work " as a requirement for all employees.

Jan became friends on a social level with one of her DRs, Irene. This friendship reached a point where Jan and her husband took vacations with Irene and her husband.

A few years down the line, Irene experienced marital problems and started a pattern of not showing up to work on time. As a result, there were grumblings about Irene's habitual tardiness. Irene's behavior was clearly in conflict with the written Organization Culture Statement Jan and her DRs, including Irene, had developed.

When the other DRs pointed out Irene's tardiness to Jan, Jan defended Irene. But, she also agreed to a meeting with all the other members of her SLT (with the exception of Irene). At the meeting, Jan explained that Irene was going through a "problem period," one that, "with a little luck," would be resolved soon. A strained silence concluded the meeting.

The next day, one of the other DRs, Beverly, asked Jan for a private meeting. She told Jan that Irene's lateness was out of hand, lasting for more than three months. She pointed out that everyone on the executive team knew that Jan was making excuses for Irene's tardiness, and that they felt Jan would not have made these excuses for any other employee, much less a senior manager. Beverly pointed out that Jan's credibility was suffering because she had created a written Culture Statement and was allowing her "friend" to violate it. Beverly also explained this double standard had led not only to deep resentment among the DRs, but to a potentially serious morale problem throughout the organization because she was allowing Irene to violate the rules others had to abide by. "That's not the culture you said you wanted around here," Beverly said.

Beverly said Jan had to "walk the walk" or no one would pay any attention to the Organization Culture Statement. Beverly kept the discussion professional, reminding Jan of her obligations to reinforce the desired organization culture.

Jan saw the light. To her surprise, she found it wasn't as hard as she expected to explain to Irene that there would no longer be an exception for her. Jan met privately with Irene and told her that while she valued her friendship, Irene was no longer free to come in late in the morning. No excuses. No exceptions. A continued pattern of lateness would mean Irene would need to find employment elsewhere. The conversation was not easy, but it was one that needed to happen, and it allowed everyone to move forward in a constructive way.

The productive workplace culture was undermined when Jan allowed a double standard to create a conflict between "what we say we do here" and "what we really do here." The productive workplace culture was restored when Jan acted to support the cultural values she wanted to sustain.

A double standard in an organization is clear evidence of an unaligned culture — a mismatch between the stated, desired culture and the actual culture. Even as you are seeking to *fix a problem* that relates to workplace culture, it is essential to *focus on* the workplace culture behavior you wish for your organization.

Cultural Misalignment/Dysfunction May be found in Surprising Places

One DR mentioned to me that his company's owner had a facilities policy that specified all equipment was to look great and be kept in top working order at all times. But in practice, he only cared about equipment within four-hundred-and-fifty feet of his office and the offices of senior management. The rest of the company's equipment did not have to meet this high standard. As a result, the business owner saw a smoothly running operation that rewarded technical excellence. However, most of his employees saw a culture that accepted neglect and carelessness with equipment. There was a collapse in trust that causes employees to "opt out" of the proclaimed organization culture instead of supporting it.

This was an example of a cultural mismatch concerning company views about equipment standards. One DR mentioned the cultural misalignment at a SLT meeting, bringing the misalignment out in the open. This was a key step in creating a positive cultural alignment throughout the organization.

If your organization is experiencing an **unaligned, dysfunctional workplace culture**, it is like **rain pouring in through the hole in your roof.** There eventually comes a Cultural Moment of Truth involving a situation where you must decide whether or not you are willing to fix the hole in the cultural roof. Cultural holes left unattended only grow bigger, never smaller. The roof will always be strongest if the KDM and DRs decide to patch the leak *together*.

Create A Written Culture Statement

One of the best things you can do to bring about an aligned culture is to create a written Organization Culture Statement. Written Organization Culture Statements have helped move many organizations from being underachievers to major forces in the business landscape. Your organization written Organization Culture Statement should reflect values and other factors you desire for an aligned culture within your business.

The KDM, with the help of the DRs, is responsible for developing a written Organization Culture Statement that can be easy for employees to use to guide workplace cultural behaviors. There should be at least one or more clear values expressed in your written Organization Culture Statement: The KDM is the primary party responsible for identifying these values, and the organization DRs collectively are the driving force responsible for the values being handed down through every layer of your organization. These identified values should be those viewed as essential to continued and increased organization success.

The Core Values you identify for your organization will become the most important workplace behavior expectations. The behaviors often identified in organization culture statements include such behaviors as:

- How employees are to be treated;
- The way employees are expected to interact with customers, prospects and others who are important to the organization;
- The way employees are expected to interact with other employees, such as honest, open, constructive discussions, engagement in teamwork and cross-functional cooperation between employees.

Your written Organization Culture Statement needs to address what is right for your organization even if it would not apply to what SLT members would want for most of their organizations. The huge on-line retailer Zappos.com, now owned by Amazon.com, used to be a much smaller, private business. One of the breakthroughs in that company's history came when the founder, Tony Hsieh, considered the top contributors in his company and asked himself what values those people had in common from a company-culture standpoint. Hsieh created a powerful written summary of his company's driving cultural values — by taking a "snapshot" of the values that were *already supporting* his company.

Zappos's extraordinary success in the years since has often been attributed to the organization culture that emerged from the successful reinforcement, and the daily expression, of those values. The following written values constitute Zappos's culture:

- Deliver WOW Through Service
- Embrace and Drive Change
- Create Fun and A Little Weirdness
- Be Adventurous, Creative, and Open-Minded
- Pursue Growth and Learning
- Build Open and Honest Relationships With Communication
- Build a Positive Team and Family Spirit

- Do More With Less
- Be Passionate and Determined
- Be Humble

It's worth noticing that Hsieh worked in the opposite direction from many company leaders in creating a cultural document. **He looked for what was already working in the company and then identified the existing positive values he wanted to reinforce and champion as the core of the workplace culture.**

Think of employees who best exemplify "what this organization is all about," and then list the qualities you associate with those people.

He had specific role models to point to for the standards he wanted everyone to follow. He made sure the company's stated values were also its behavioral values. It was not just talk. If you work for Zappos and you consistently fail to uphold one or more of these values, you can be terminated for not supporting the company culture.

The following are some of the questions that you and your SLT should consider when determining values for your written Organization Culture Statement:

- Is there a value relating to integrity/honesty/work ethic or respect?
- Is there a value relating to the way employees work with other employees, such as not talking about them behind their backs?
- Is there a value relating to timeliness and meeting deadlines/ commitments?
- Is there a value relating to respectful conflict resolution?
- Is there a value relating to employee development/training/continuing education?

Full Cooperation and Respectful Conflict Resolution Among Employees

An organization whose leadership emphasizes that all employees must make a strong commitment to meet or exceed the expectations of their internal customers (fellow employees) is more likely to generate high external customer satisfaction scores than an organization with a culture in which employees view internal customers as rivals or obstacles.

According to Professors Ken Thompson (DePaul University) and Fred Luthans (University of Nebraska), **Culture Is Learned Through Interaction.** We learn our most important lessons about workplace culture when we interact with other employees. We usually figure out what the culture is, and how we can fit into it, based on the exchanges we have with other people.

This means it is up to the SLT to make it clear that things like sarcasm, backbiting, gossiping and jokes that come at the expense of other people will not be acceptable because they have negative effects on the work environment. You need to make it clear that your organization culture requires "Teamwork and Cross Functional Cooperation."

Conflict of some kind is inevitable in any organization, which is why a productive workplace culture is dependent on resolving conflicts respectfully. This, like most cultural matters, must be demonstrated at the top. KDMs and DRs must model effective conflict resolution for the rest of the organization. The ability to use and model effective conflict resolution techniques is important to the productive working culture of the organization as a whole.

Without meaningful efforts from both sides to resolve the most difficult conflicts, the KDM and DR will not have the trust necessary to give full effort towards achieving goals set by the KDM.

Successful conflict resolution depends on taking the time to understand each other's true motives, patience, and the assumption of good intent on both sides. Make sure there are plenty of all these elements on your side when you get into a conflict.

Dianne, a DR, mentioned to me that her boss, Carlos, was "paranoid" as he was always asking her whether one of the other employees was doing something against his direction. She felt that Carlos had, at times, also treated her with suspicion. When she decided to explain to Carlos that she had his back no matter how she felt about some of his decisions, he reacted in a loud, threatening voice that he was being undermined. As might be expected, she shared his reaction with many employees. It's not surprising that other DRs learned to do the things Carlos did in conflict situations, and the culture of the organization reflected this value from top to bottom.

When the relationship is based on mutual respect, and mutual commitment, then differing perspectives and points of view become much easier to address without the type of reaction Carlos displayed. This takes discipline and commitment to the value of effective conflict resolution.

> *A commitment to mutual respect among organization employees starts with the KDM/DR relationship as the foundation upon which all positive cultural experiences and expectations within the rest of the organization are built.*

Sometimes, even with plenty of goodwill and patience, effective conflict resolution may require the involvement of a neutral third party from outside your organization. If a neutral third party is needed, try to identify someone who understands your organization well enough to facilitate discussions based upon the business realities of your particular organization.

Communication Commitment Exercises Help Create a Safe Communication Environment

One technique for bringing about respect and openness of communications among your employees is the use of Communication Commitment exercises, which I will explain in more detail shortly. These exercises will help create an atmosphere in which your employees feel safe to communicate their thoughts. This methodology will help avoid disrespectful, counter-productive communication.

These Communication Commitment exercises are done in a series of workshops focused on communications culture. The first such meeting is where The Communication Commitment exercises are conducted with the KDM and all the DRs within the SLT. Once this culture is established at the top, each DR needs to have similar group meetings that extend down to every level of the organization.

The result of these exercises is to create an environment where employees can express their views in an open and honest manner without retaliation or negative communication behaviors such as aggressive/sarcastic tone and raised voices. Another byproduct of the Communication Commitment exercises is that employees at all levels of the organization will feel that their ideas will be heard.

These Communication Commitment meetings are most effective when run by a facilitator who understands and knows how to use the Communication Commitment exercises. The facilitator starts by explaining the objective of the exercises, which is to develop an understanding of how to successfully communicate in an environment that allows for safe, honest and open communication. The facilitator then explains that he or she will ask for responses to three questions. This will be followed by a commitment from all in the meeting to certain types of communications with other employees.

The facilitator then starts the exercises by calling on each participant to respond with one word or a small phrase to the question. The facilitator then writes the responses on a whiteboard, blackboard or computer monitor projector so that all participants may see the responses.

The first question asked is, "What type of communication, verbal or non-verbal, may cause you or others to become defensive?" Common answers include such things as someone using sarcasm, avoiding eye contact, being silent, responding defensively, changing the subject, making cynical remarks, objecting without thinking things through or outright lying.

The second question asked is, "How would you describe what a 'safe, honest and open' communication environment looks like?" Common responses include, "There are no hidden agendas," "People respect all ideas," "We all try to find common ground," and "We all try to give positive feedback or constructive criticism."

The third question asked is, "Can you describe a benefit that will be gained when communicating is done in a safe, open and respectful atmosphere?" Common responses include, "I feel safe to express my ideas to others," "I get more ideas from others," "I feel I have a support system," and "I feel as if we can trust one another."

The next step involves asking for a communication commitment. The facilitator asks the participants to look at each of the responses to the previous questions. After the wording has been clarified and deletions made, the facilitator will ask participants if they are willing to give a verbal commitment to adhere to the communication behavior culture identified in the responses or whether there are any to which they disagree. The facilitator will also ask participants to commit to pointing out any behavior that violates the commitments. Participants may ask for a clarification of the responses before giving a commitment or may express any disagreements they may have. After discussions, the list will undergo tweaking to reflect the discussion.

The results of the meeting, including the responses to the questions and the commitment made by all participants, should be distributed in writing to all participants. You will see immediate benefits in the way of improved employee communication. However, to make this improvement long-term, it is important to review the exercises annually. This is because some communication patterns formed within the year might not have been present before, and also the communication dynamics have changed because new employees are now involved.

The following is an example of what was sent out by one company to group participants who went through the exercises.

"We, the management group for Parker Technologies, have discussed the desire to create a communications atmosphere in which employees feel safe in expressing their views in an open manner. We believe that living up to this communications culture will help our company achieve greater success while at the same time making the work experience less stressful and more enjoyable for company employees. Together, our discussions have discovered the following conditions that may exist and agree to recognize the following:"

- Conditions that contribute to raising our defenses, which in turn prevent effective communications:

Non-participation	*Purposely wasting time*
Contrarian always in opposition	*Illogical, unemotional responses*
Pedantic	*Being habitually late to meetings*
Dishonesty	*Exaggeration*

Public criticism (berating)
No discussion
Intentional deception
Questioning ethics and sincerity
Condescending responses
Mistrust

Negativity creating barriers
Overemotional responses
Pettiness
Uneducated responses
Hollow excuses
Personal attacks

- Conditions that have to be present at meetings for our employees to feel safe so they can act in an honest and open manner:

Absence of hidden agendas
Sincerity
Openness
No fear
Non-judgmental atmosphere
Win-win atmosphere

Know each other (develops over time)
Trust
Neutral environment
Guidelines for conduct
Goal-oriented discussions

- The following benefits will take place if we use communications behavior consistent with the above responses:

Foundation to build upon
Build trust
Greater understanding
Increased leadership development
Resolution of problems
Group growth
Reduction of the common stress

Greater effort
New and creative ideas
Personal growth
Business will run more effectively
Better understanding of problems
Synergy
Working together towards common goals

- *"The parties who have signed below commit to using the communications behaviors identified above and to 'call out' any employee who violates the communications commitment"*

Integrity

Let's see what integrity looks like in practice within an organization. Integrity means adherence to moral and ethical principles, soundness of moral character and honesty. Each employee operating with a viewpoint of "does my action reflect integrity?" is critical to honoring this core cultural value. There are ways that integrity, or lack thereof, consistently comes into play within all organizations.

One way integrity is demonstrated is through accountability to meet and fulfill time commitments. This starts with your organization KDM/

> *Build a culture value where the person committing to the timeline will either accomplish what they say they will by the promised date, or ask for help.*

DRs setting an example. An organization that tolerates a team or individual's consistent inability to meet commitments is an organization that won't maximize its opportunity for success. Your employees must understand that your organization culture and values require they keep their commitment. This includes meeting their committed-to deadlines. It also includes keeping less important day-to-day commitments. Employees should be able to count on their fellow employees to not allow things to fall through the cracks.

Simply stated, your organization employees shouldn't make commitments unless they fully intend to keep them. An organization culture that supports and rewards meeting deadlines helps employees organize their time and set their priorities. Meeting deadlines makes the organization more efficient while also giving employees a sense of satisfaction.

For subordinate employees to meet their deadlines, managers need to have the discipline to stick to one set of established priorities before moving to the next. The emphasis is on mutually respecting (or, in extreme cases, renegotiating) scheduled commitments, which is a value that some, particularly very creative leaders, sometimes find difficult to embrace.

Deadline problems take place when priorities change too frequently. This could be because someone with delegating authority has come up with a new idea and resets priorities after having already assigned an employee or team a different priority. The subordinate employee or

> *If one of your employees has a pattern of not keeping commitment deadlines, the organization culture will be affected in an adverse way, as will the organization results.*

team may have committed to a deadline under the original assignment and the next thing they know, the manager is on to the next idea with the individual/team being told to work on something relating to the new idea. This type of leadership can contribute significantly to creating a culture where employees feel that deadlines are meaningless.

Your employees should never mislead people intentionally, whether other employees or clients/customers. If they don't know something, they should say, " I don't know." Your employees shouldn't say things they don't mean, and they shouldn't play games with other people's expectations of them.

If your word means nothing in "little" situations, how much will it be worth in "big" situations?

To put it another way, your employees' words and their actions should be in full Alignment. This applies to unimportant and important matters.

Your SLT must make it known that it is very important for employees to operate in alignment with the value of integrity. Their daily actions are evidence they are living in alignment with integrity.

Will your employees slip up sometimes? Probably — they are human. So will you. When you give your word, mean what you say. When you commit to something, make sure you keep your commitment, or, failing that, circle back to the person you made the commitment to and explain why you can't keep your commitment. When you slip up, you'll need to apologize where appropriate and do your best to make amends to those you've let down. If that's not the standard you're willing to hold yourself to, you should not expect your employees to take your requirement of integrity seriously.

Other Values

In addition to the values already discussed in this chapter, the following are a couple of examples of other values for your organization to consider:

- All employees welcome/embrace change
- Our employees will provide the level of service that produces loyal customers
- All employees are passionate about the work that they do

Organization Culture Factors That Are Organization-Philosophy Based and Not Dependent On Behavior Of Employees

There are some things in your Culture Statement that will reflect the philosophy of your SLT rather than expected behavior of your employees. In some organizations, it is the philosophy toward paying employees. An example of this would be: "We will try to pay our employees at the high level of what is paid for someone with comparable experience and ability in our marketplace. Another example is a commitment to respect employee views, which include such things as getting employee weigh-in on certain matters.

One factor I have seen in some Organization Culture Statements, that I think should be in all organizations, is the factor of desiring and helping employee professional development. Many highly successful organizations feel strongly about committing to ongoing employee development as an investment that can have a huge impact on the organization's long-term success. They view this investment as one that will help an employee develop to his/her highest potential for maximum positive impact on the organization.

The final list of "cultural values" should be ones that your KDM and DRs share and can personally model for the rest of the enterprise.

An organization that does not value employee development creates a culture that drives away high-impact performers. Employees invariably choose to pursue other employment options whenever they have the opportunity to grow. In contrast, an organization that encourages and supports employee professional growth will have a major competitive edge when recruiting employees as well as in retaining high-impact employees.

A few years ago, after I gave a business presentation to the public, I happened to meet Julio — a DR-level manger who explained he had recently quit an organization where he had worked for nearly a decade. He told me he had raised the issue with his KDM many times of the organization paying for an online MBA. His KDM responded by saying the organization had no business making such investments. He did not consider the potential dollar value of the many years of institutional experience that walked out the door with Julio. I suspect the cost to the organization was much more than the tuition of the MBA program Julio wanted to take. Also, when a long-term employee quits, it

> *Employee efficiency and organization success are profoundly affected by an organization's commitment to continuing education and professional development. This can have a significant impact on the organization's long-term growth.*

often has serious, negative moral implications for the organization.

For this culture to be embraced by employees, it is important the KDM makes it clear that the organization has embraced this culture and has made a financial and time commitment to it. Your KDM and DRs should be prepared to discuss ways and paths for your employees to develop and grow within the organization.

Reading books like this one, by the way, are excellent ways for your managers to gain personal development. Another method of personal development is taking online training courses paid for by employers when the courses are satisfactorily completed. These courses are typically restricted to ones that are relevant to both the employee's career path and the competitiveness of your enterprise. We are blessed to live in a time when it is extremely easy to find relatively inexpensive, good online programs, ranging from management development training programs to programs focused on particular skills, such as using a certain type of software.

Conclusion

A strong Organization Culture Statement reflects values and other factors that fuel a strong workplace. A strong workplace will fuel strong organization growth. Invest the time to identify and communicate what you want your aligned organization culture to look like. Then take the actions needed to make it happen.

SECTION 3

Organization Diagnostic and Critical Success Factors

One evening, I was celebrating with a professional turnaround specialist and CEO who had just sold his company. Several years earlier, he led the company from the brink of bankruptcy to one with a seven-figure annual net income. He had previously accomplished the same type of success with several other turnaround situations. I asked him what his secrets for success were in these turnaround situations. He said the first secret was that he didn't make any important decisions or plans until he completed an organization diagnostic.

Regardless as to how successful or unsuccessful your organization is, you should not start creating your Strategic Plans until you have done a diagnostic of your organization. These reviews are needed before creating organization plans, so that the plans lead your organization to its greatest potential for success. There are three steps that collectively make up the organization diagnostic.

The first step is to answer an organization diagnostic questionnaire. The second step is the SWOT. The preplanning diagnostic evaluation that many organization people refer to as a "SWOT" evaluation, consists of a very objective and honest look at your organization and assessing it for each of the following:

- Your organization's **S**trengths
- Your organization's **W**eaknesses
- Your organization's **O**pportunities
- Your organization's **T**hreats

The purpose of doing an organization diagnostic is so your organization KDM and DRs can gain essential insights by assessing the organization from a comprehensive, analytical perspective.

The third step is to identify your Organization Critical Success Factors.

I will discuss each of these steps in the following chapters.

CHAPTER 5

The Organization Diagnostic Questionnaire

The organization diagnostic questionnaire is a list of questions that, if answered by all your SLT members, will give thought-provoking answers with great insight into your organization. These answers will, in turn, help you identify the strengths, weaknesses, opportunities and threats for your organization SWOT, which is the second step in your organization diagnostic work. I will discuss SWOT statements and how to use them, in the next chapter.

Below are examples of the type of questions that should be answered by all members of your SLT before your team meets to create organization SWOT statements and to determine your organization Critical Success Factors. Not all of the categories of questions below are likely to be of equal importance to your organization, and some, such as the family-business-related questions, may not apply to your organization. Your SLT should be able to come up with additional questions relevant to your organization.

Planning

- The organization holds effective strategic planning sessions.
  (strongly disagree) 0 1 2 3 4 5 6 7 8 9 10 (strongly agree)

- A clearly written organization vision has been established.
  (strongly disagree) 0 1 2 3 4 5 6 7 8 9 10 (strongly agree)

- Our organization prioritizes all our strategic goals by how they impact the organization's critical success factors.
  (strongly disagree) 0 1 2 3 4 5 6 7 8 9 10 (strongly agree)

Employee Development

- The organization effectively motivates employees to achieve goals.
  (strongly disagree) 0 1 2 3 4 5 6 7 8 9 10 (strongly agree)

- Most people who work here feel fulfilled.
  (strongly disagree) 0 1 2 3 4 5 6 7 8 9 10 (strongly agree)

- Our organization measures employee performance objectively and has effective performance evaluations.
  (strongly disagree) 0 1 2 3 4 5 6 7 8 9 10 (strongly agree)

Marketing

- The organization marketing is effective at raising awareness and generating interest in our products and services.
  (strongly disagree) 0 1 2 3 4 5 6 7 8 9 10 (strongly agree)

- Our organization utilizes all relevant marketing channels effectively and measures results using metrics.
  (strongly disagree) 0 1 2 3 4 5 6 7 8 9 10 (strongly agree)

- Our organization knows how we are differentiated from our competition.
  (strongly disagree) 0 1 2 3 4 5 6 7 8 9 10 (strongly agree)

Sales

- The organization trains its salespeople well.
  (strongly disagree) 0 1 2 3 4 5 6 7 8 9 10 (strongly agree)

- The organization has a well-documented and well-communicated selling process.
  (strongly disagree) 0 1 2 3 4 5 6 7 8 9 10 (strongly agree)

- Our organization has identified and measured key sales metrics (leads, sales, sales cycle time, re-orders, etc.).
  (strongly disagree) 0 1 2 3 4 5 6 7 8 9 10 (strongly agree)

Internal Communications

- All employees are updated on the performance and future of the organization.
  (strongly disagree) 0 1 2 3 4 5 6 7 8 9 10 (strongly agree)

- Managers find it easy to get the information they need to complete key tasks.
  (strongly disagree) 0 1 2 3 4 5 6 7 8 9 10 (strongly agree)

- We believe that our employees are entitled to a wide range of organization information, including financials.
  (strongly disagree) 0 1 2 3 4 5 6 7 8 9 10 (strongly agree)

Customer Service

- Employees service both internal and external customers well.
  (strongly disagree) 0 1 2 3 4 5 6 7 8 9 10 (strongly agree)

- The organization utilizes service metrics and evaluates the service it delivers from the customer's perspective.
  (strongly disagree) 0 1 2 3 4 5 6 7 8 9 10 (strongly agree)

- We have a customer relationship management (CRM) system to track service issues and sales.
  (strongly disagree) 0 1 2 3 4 5 6 7 8 9 10 (strongly agree)

Operations

- The organization has developed and is following effective internal procedures to operate the organization.
  (strongly disagree) 0 1 2 3 4 5 6 7 8 9 10 (strongly agree)

- Internal procedures are clearly documented and as a result the organization operates effectively.
  (strongly disagree) 0 1 2 3 4 5 6 7 8 9 10 (strongly agree)

- Our employees are empowered to make important business decisions especially those related to customer satisfaction.
  (strongly disagree) 0 1 2 3 4 5 6 7 8 9 10 (strongly agree)

Information Technology

- Critical business data is secure against disaster.
  (strongly disagree) 0 1 2 3 4 5 6 7 8 9 10 (strongly agree)

- Managers have easy access to critical business data.
  (strongly disagree) 0 1 2 3 4 5 6 7 8 9 10 (strongly agree)

- Most information processes have been automated.
  (strongly disagree) 0 1 2 3 4 5 6 7 8 9 10 (strongly agree)

Corporate Finances

- The organization has an effective process for developing and communicating internal financial information to those who use it to guide decision making.
  (strongly disagree) 0 1 2 3 4 5 6 7 8 9 10 (strongly agree)

- The organization's capital resources are allocated effectively.
  (strongly disagree) 0 1 2 3 4 5 6 7 8 9 10 (strongly agree)

- Our organization has a purchase order system for all supplies and materials.
  (strongly disagree) 0 1 2 3 4 5 6 7 8 9 10 (strongly agree)

Human Resources Procedures

- The organization recruits employees effectively.
  (strongly disagree) 0 1 2 3 4 5 6 7 8 9 10 *(strongly agree)*

- The organization does a good job of retaining key people.
  (strongly disagree) 0 1 2 3 4 5 6 7 8 9 10 *(strongly agree)*

- Exit interviews are conducted and all feedback is shared effectively.
  (strongly disagree) 0 1 2 3 4 5 6 7 8 9 10 *(strongly agree)*

Alignment

- We hold effective strategic team planning sessions that clarify long-term priorities.
  (strongly disagree) 0 1 2 3 4 5 6 7 8 9 10 *(strongly agree)*

- We hold regular staff meetings to plan and review short-term priorities.
  (strongly disagree) 0 1 2 3 4 5 6 7 8 9 10 *(strongly agree)*

- Everyone's daily priorities are clear.
  (strongly disagree) 0 1 2 3 4 5 6 7 8 9 10 *(strongly agree)*

Family Business (If Your Organization Is A Family Business)

- All family members understand and agree on the vision for the organization.
  (strongly disagree) 0 1 2 3 4 5 6 7 8 9 10 *(strongly agree)*

- We understand the behavioral styles, skills and experience of each family member and have analyzed what they bring to the team.
  (strongly disagree) 0 1 2 3 4 5 6 7 8 9 10 *(strongly agree)*

- Each family member has signed a Family Business Participation Agreement outlining the separation of work and family relationships and the responsibilities of spouses of family members.
  (strongly disagree) 0 1 2 3 4 5 6 7 8 9 10 *(strongly agree)*

> *Don't be surprised if there is an enormous variance between the ways different SLT members answer the questions. This is usually a very revealing process.*

Try, whenever possible, to describe your answers in a measurable manner by comparing your organization to others in your industry. For some of the questions, you will be able to find relevant industry-specific statistics to which you can compare your organization's performance. You can get a great amount of industry-specific comparison information from your trade organization and other sources found on the Internet.

You Are Now Ready For Creating Organization SWOT Statements

Once your team has completed discussions of the answers to the questionnaire, you will be ready for the second step of your Organization Diagnostic — creating written SWOT statements.

CHAPTER 6

Organization SWOT Analysis

The second step in your organization diagnostic is to complete a SWOT analysis, which will culminate in written SWOT Statements. SWOT refers to the pre-planning diagnostic evaluation for:

- Your organization's **S**trengths
- Your organization's **W**eaknesses
- Your organization's **O**pportunities
- Your organization's **T**hreats

Do not make key decisions or start creating formal organization plans until you have completed SWOT evaluations of your organization, making use of the answers given to the Questionnaire referred to in the first step. The SWOT evaluations should result in written SWOT Statements that will help your organization identify the most critical factors that must be satisfied to achieve desired success. A SWOT evaluation is also helpful in creating realistic, strategically focused organization plans that best utilize your organization strengths, neutralize any weaknesses, take advantage of opportunities and react to threats outside your control.

The road to business success is rarely flat. At times, your organization will have to climb hills that seem daunting. But, if your organization SWOT evaluation shows the hills can realistically be climbed, you can create plans to reach the top, and the hills ahead will seem far less intimidating. Your Organization SWOT Statements will also help your organization avoid taking any route that leads to insurmountable hills.

It is important to have an objective view of your current business situation before you make decisions to change things. One way to keep it less emotional is to start the SWOT analysis by focusing on functions and not so much on the individuals.

Among other benefits, the SWOT evaluation will give you an idea of what is realistically attainable. When SWOT diagnostic principles are used before making your organization planning decisions, you know "what fences need to be moved and to what location."

It is demoralizing and a waste of organization financial and human assets when you set in motion a plan that is not realistically attainable. After considering the results of your SWOT analysis, you may even see the need to revise your written Organization Vision Statement.

Some of your SWOT evaluations will be subjective, with different SLT members seeing the same things very differently. Some factors in your organization SWOT can be based upon empirical evidence, such as from sales results or survey data. It is now very inexpensive to do web-based surveys, to assess what your employees, customers and suppliers think about your organization's Strengths, Weaknesses, Opportunities and Threats.

> *DRs should challenge all factors of organization SWOT statements presented by the KDM to which they do not agree.*

In most organizations, the SWOT review discussions will start with the SWOT factors as seen through the eyes of the KDM. All members of your SLT should give your Organization SWOT Statements a "devil's advocate" review and also share their respective observations.

Now let's look at each factor in the SWOT at a much deeper level, starting with (S) Strengths.

(S) Organization Strengths

Strengths refer to the areas in which your organization excels. The process of identifying your Organization Strengths Statement is usually enjoyable because this statement contains the "good stuff." Organization Strengths are the easiest organization factors to leverage when creating plans to achieve improved organization results.

Not everyone on the SLT may view the same things as organization strengths

The KDM of a manufacturing organization identified the organization's marketing department as one of the organization's Strengths. She stated the department "is outstanding." The KDM was deeply involved in organization marketing activities.

Her DRs did not agree with her view of marketing being an organization Strength. They explained they believed it was actually an organization Weakness. One of the reasons given was that the organization spent far too high a percentage of annual revenue on marketing compared to others in the same manufacturing field, based upon trade association information.

Organization Strengths

Identify your organization Strengths by answering the questions below as they relate to your organization. The questions are not intended to be all encompassing, and, in fact, some of the questions may not apply at all to your organization. The purpose of the questions is to stimulate your evaluative thinking. Your SLT may come up with questions not included in my list. Look at each section of questions below and add questions that will help your organization identify its greatest Strengths.

Strengths of Management or Departments

- What departments have outstanding performance?
- What employees who report to DRs have demonstrated outstanding ability to grow in importance to the organization?

- Does the organization have outstanding competencies in such areas as strategic thinking, innovative thinking, technological savviness, team building acumen, customer relations, innovative use of resources, communication skills, problem solving, mentoring ability or great leadership?

Financial Factors

- Does your organization have little to no outstanding long-term debt?
- What patents or other intellectual property and/or trademarked services does your organization own?
- Does your organization have a strong cash position?

Sales and marketing

- Does your sales staff excel at selling organization products/services?
- Does your organization have an outstanding sales system?
- Does your organization have marketing methods or tools that are extremely effective in getting sales leads?

Manufacturing, Operations and Distribution

- Does your organization have a low-cost manufacturing process?
- Does your organization have up-to-date and efficient information systems?
- Is your organization certified by the International Organization for Standardization (ISO)?
- What are your organization's most effective outlets/distribution channels?

Products/Services

- Are your products/services of higher quality when compared to competitors?

- Are your organization products/services innovative?
- Are your organization products/services the price leaders?

KDM's Strengths

- Is there a special skill of your KDM that is outstanding?

KDM Strengths

The degree of importance of a KDM's strength in relation to your organization Strengths usually varies with the size of your organization. In a small, privately owned organization, your KDM's business skills are likely to be disproportionately essential to the success of the organization. The more employees in your organization, the less dependence there typically is on a KDM's specific business skills.

Once your SLT have written down answers to these questions, the facilitator of your meeting should request a discussion of each answer to make sure most of the team is satisfied that the answers clearly represent your current Organization Strengths.

Start Writing Your Organization Strengths Statement

Once you have answered the applicable Organization Strength evaluation questions, consider the importance of each of your answers. Your Organization Strengths have different degrees of potential positive impact for your organization to reach the future you desire. Finalize the Strengths to no more than five that have the most potential to positively impact your organization's ability to reach that future. Your formal written Organization Strengths Statement should only contain the Strengths that have the most potential for the greatest impact.

The following is an example of a Strengths Statement of a manufacturing business:

- Experienced management and manufacturing personnel;
- We have a well-documented manufacturing process and systems;
- We own patents on certain products and parts;

- The owner's knowledge of quality construction methods;
- The manufacturing plant has room for a great amount of expansion.

Now that you understand how to identify your Organization Strengths, we're ready to look at Organization Weaknesses.

(W) Organization Weaknesses

Organization Weaknesses are factors that have been causing your organization to underachieve, compared to its potential. Looking at your organization's Weaknesses isn't always a "cake walk," and you may not like seeing the realities of the critical shortcomings of your organization. However, you can't neutralize a Weakness without first identifying it.

> *Recognizing a problem doesn't always bring a solution, but until we recognize that problem, there can be no solution.*
>
> — **JAMES BALDWIN**

Your SLT must objectively identify what they actually see in the organization, not what they wish to see. Identifying your Organization Weaknesses is like finding defective parts on your bike before you take a ride — you make the repairs or replace the parts so that your bike runs well, does not break down or leave you stranded on the road to success. Those who fail to consider their Organization Weaknesses before creating their organization plans often find their organization plans break down before they reach their desired destination.

Organization Weaknesses

Even the most successful organizations have Organization Weaknesses. You now have to look at the organization's weaknesses, in addition to your Personal Organization Weaknesses, that can have "Big Picture" impact. The following are starter questions to help you explore your Organization Weaknesses. When you answer the questions, avoid using long narratives to explain or justify any Weaknesses. The key is to pinpoint the problems. In the following chapters, you will learn how to develop Organization Plans that either remedy or neutralize Organization Weaknesses.

Management and Other Personnel

- Does your organization have thin management infrastructure, a lack of management structure or lack of clarity of roles?
- Does your management have a culture of non-accountability? Ignoring repeated violations is an endorsement of an undesirable culture. Keeping employees who violate accountability and fight positive change will destroy a culture.
- Are there any areas where management lacks skills that hinder organization success? (E.g. communication skills, ineffective decision making, lack of innovation.)
- What shortcomings exist among your personnel in terms of skills or competencies? Consider factors such as technological skill deficiency, inability to follow directions, lack of initiative, or uncooperative attitude.
- Do you have employees who resist change? These employees generally don't come out and say they don't support something — they just don't do it. When you have resistant employees, you need to move them out of your organization or get a commitment that their behavior will change.
- Do your organization departments work well together in a spirit of alignment? Picture being in a rowboat with others and one person is rowing in the wrong direction, or at a different speed, or with different timing. The result is inefficient forward momentum. This exemplifies a common, though significant, Weakness in many organizations — lack of alignment. Many times organizations don't succeed with their plans because they think their employees are rowing their oars in the same direction when they're not. This can be a serious Weakness.

Financial Factors

- Does your organization have a poor cash flow?
- Does your organization have an inability to increase line of credit?
- Is your fixed overhead very high?

Sales and marketing

- Are your marketing materials old and/or ineffective?
- Is your cost of marketing to sales high compared to others in your industry?
- What aspects of your sales process are least effective?

Manufacturing, Operations and Distribution

- What operational issues keep your organization from operating efficiently?
- Do you need to increase or decrease the number of cities in which you sell your product/service?
- Is your cost of manufacturing high compared to others in your industry?

Products/Services

- Are any of your products and/or services vulnerable to product/service substitution or commoditization?
- What, or who, in your organization is responsible for product or service failure?
- What quality control issues does your organization have?
- Is there a technological advantage your competitors' products/services have over yours?

KDM Weaknesses

- Is the organization overly dependent upon the KDM?

- Does the KDM have a weakness, such as not being good at driving a project or plan, that strongly impacts the organization?
- Does the KDM change priorities on a frequent (e.g. weekly) basis?

KDM Weakness

One of the hardest aspects of doing a Weakness diagnostic is discussing weaknesses of the KDM. It's not hard if the weaknesses are something like organization overdependence on the KDM for generating new business. However, if the weakness is something like "the KDM is not good at driving a project or plan", that can be more difficult to discuss.

Paul, the owner of one company, had a dream of doubling the size of his technology consulting division within five years. It didn't happen. The problem that prevented it was Paul's inability to strategically lead the company. When I met with Kevin, Paul's Executive Vice President, he explained his view that Paul is not an effective leader. Kevin mentioned that Paul was constantly caught up in handling day-to-day matters and didn't give the necessary time to lead the company's major initiatives, which requires focus over a period of months, or even years. Kevin talked about how tough things were on a typical day for him, and other executives, because of Paul's spur-of-the-moment involvement in day-to-day matters without any strategic thinking.

I asked Kevin if he or any other member of his SLT had ever approached Paul about the problem. "Oh, I've tried." Kevin sighed. "But Paul doesn't see the truth of how ineffectively he operates."

When talking to Paul prior to the SLT meeting to discuss the Organization Weaknesses Statement, I asked Paul to list his Personal Organization Weaknesses. His list showed he recognized his personal weaknesses because they included:

- Lack of self accountability
- Weak at strategic leadership

Paul expressed to me that while he was really good at technological innovation and solving specific project problems, he knew he was not good at following through with scheduled strategic planning meetings. He said he cancelled or postponed most of them because of more pressing matters.

When I mentioned this should be discussed openly at the team SWOT meeting, he said he didn't want to share this with his team. Only the KDM can decide which Personal Organization Weaknesses he or she is willing to share with some, or all, of the SLT. Fortunately, after a lot of discussion, Paul agreed to be open about this subject with the SLT. At the SLT meeting on Organization Weaknesses, he stated, "I get too caught up in handling day-to-day matters." Only after this acknowledgement was the company able to develop a plan to overcome the negative impact of Paul's Personal Organization Weakness.

Later in this book, I will show you how to develop Organization Plans that will result in eliminating or minimizing work Weaknesses that have the potential for "Big Picture" negative impact on your organization.

Organization Weaknesses Statement Example

Let's take a look at items listed in one organization's written Organization Weaknesses Statement:

- Poor customer service per internal feedback surveys from management and non-management employees;
- Sales training and sales training materials are poor;
- Sales department lacks a sales manager;
- Do not have a sales methodology;
- Top domestic salesperson has been diverted to international sales;
- Poor marketing materials;
- Less brand awareness than competitors;
- Too dependent upon a costly outside marketing firm;
- Corporate website copy and messaging is weak;
- Poor project management with poor execution of new product development;
- There is a lack of capable supervisory backups;
- No clear written organization culture.

Now Write Your Weaknesses Statement

Once you have answered the applicable Organization Weaknesses evaluation questions, consider the importance of each of your answers. Your Organization Weaknesses have different degrees of potential negative impact for your organization reaching the future you desire. Make sure the factors listed in your Organization Weaknesses Statement are limited to those that present the biggest obstacles to attaining the Organization Vision.

Now that you understand how to identify your Organization Weaknesses, we're ready to look at Organization Opportunities.

(O) Organization Opportunities

Opportunities refer to things your organization is not doing, or not using, that if embraced by your organization would help improve its level of success. Your SLT discussions of opportunity need to be done without "putting down" or criticizing any opportunity ideas when they are first brought up at the meeting. Identifying realistically attainable Opportunities for your organization is usually exciting and stimulating!

Some members of your SLT may be the ones more frequently generating ideas about new opportunities. That's OK, because not everyone has the ability to see opportunities or to think outside your industry box in order to bring new ideas into better focus. Sometimes we don't recognize opportunities because we are so ingrained with how we see our own organization and the industry in which we operate.

Sometimes, ideas come from SLT brainstorming sessions. When the light bulb goes on and you see the opportunity, you may wonder why it took so long to recognize it and feel as if it had been in front of your face waiting to be seen for a long time.

Questions to Help Identify Organization Opportunities

Your answers to the following questions will help you identify Opportunities that have the potential for the greatest positive impact on your organization.

Management and Other Personnel

- What opportunities could you take advantage of to strengthen the skills of your management team and other personnel? (E.g. online training classes, seminars and mentoring?)
- Is there potential to upgrade personnel in your organization?

Financial Factors

- What current financial opportunities exist that could potentially benefit your organization, such as refinancing real estate at a lower interest rate?
- Should capital expenditure be reallocated for uses that bring about greater financial positive impact?
- What are the worst-case/best-case budget scenarios for the opportunity ROI?
- Is there an opportunity to reduce your organization's taxes? At one time, every retail chain in Missouri was required to pay a tax on the inventory they held on a specific date every year. None of the other states had a similar tax. An organization named the "Missouri Merchants and Manufacturers Association," which was comprised of other clients of the business community, was a cohesive voice for eliminating the inventory tax. This effort ultimately resulted in a Missouri state constitutional amendment that ended the inventory tax.

Sales and marketing

- What industry trends exist that your marketing and sales efforts can leverage?
- What consumer buyer trends could have a positive impact on your organization sales?
- Is there the potential to sell additional products/services or new products/services to current customers/clients, or should the organization look to new customers?
- Can your sales process be improved to help your sales team communicate your offer?

- What strategic alliance/partner opportunities exist? (E.g. acquaintances may be interested in coming into the organization or becoming a strategic partner.)
- Is there a new technology or distribution channel to market your goods or services? (E.g. social media opened up a whole new world of marketing opportunities for many organizations.)
- What are your customers' future needs?

Manufacturing, Operations and Distribution

- What operational improvement opportunities exist for your organization?
- Are there opportunities to reduce expenses or production time?
- What new technology is available, or will soon be available, that may lower organization costs or speed production? (E.g. new software for client management.)
- Is there a need to improve or change your distribution methods?
- How do your organization's manufacturing capabilities compare to your competitors?
- What processes, if any, does your organization currently provide to your customers, clients or users that may be provided more effectively by outsourcing?
- Can you improve your procurement procedures, qualification rules and information systems for vendor management?

Products/Services

- Are your major competitors vulnerable in relationship to any specific products/services on which you can capitalize?
- What technology or market changes create a new product or service need? (E.g. a smart phone application.)
- Are there markets that could be entered into easily using the organization's current areas of excellence and capabilities?

KDM Related Opportunities

- Does the KDM have any special relationships, such as relationships with potential investors who could provide investment funds, which could be used for organization expansion?

Organization Opportunities Relating to the KDM

Opportunities that personally involve the owner may be Organization Opportunities. The smaller your organization, the more likely it will be that your KDM's related Opportunities will be potentially of great impact to your organization.

Example of an organization's Written Opportunities Statement

The following is an example of a written Organization Opportunities Statement:

- Increase brand awareness via social networks like LinkedIn and Facebook, and exhibit at targeted industry expos;
- Offer ancillary repair services to products we sell;
- Employ in-house telemarketers to set appointments with new customer prospects;
- Improve initial and continuing sales training of technical staff and upgrade technology to improve quality of products.

Now Write Your Organization Opportunities Statement

Once you have answered the applicable Organization Opportunities evaluation questions, consider the importance of each of your answers. Your Organization Opportunities have different degrees of potential positive impact for your organization reaching the future you desire. Not all Opportunities are created equal. Just because a new opportunity exists doesn't necessarily mean you should go for it. It's important to prioritize Opportunities based upon potential impact on the organization and also to consider whether your organization has the ability to capitalize on the opportunity.

Make sure the factors listed in your Organization Opportunities Statement are limited to those that present the greatest potential to move your organization forward. Do this by asking which of your Organization Opportunities have the greatest "Big Picture Potential" to reach your Organization Vision. These are the Opportunities that need to be identified in your formal written Organization Opportunities Statement.

Now that you understand how to identify your Organization Opportunities, we're ready to look at Organization Threats.

(T) Organization Threats

"Threats", as referred to in SWOT, means those things that can greatly hurt your organization but are outside your control. Threats your organization faces today, and those you may face tomorrow, can have a significant negative impact if your organization does not take timely actions.

But even though you can't stop these types of Threats from happening, you can — most of the time — identify things that will help your organization develop proactive measures to protect itself. After you recognize significant Threats to your organization, you will want to try to develop armor to protect against them.

This armor may involve significant changes in your organization's course, while at the same time preserving what is working for your organization. Sometimes Threats require reevaluation and modification of your business model.

For most Threats, actions taken in time can move your organization out of harm's way. For example, your organization has no control over whether there is a global recession, but you can tighten your organization belt on expenses to weather the recession. Another example is that your organization has no control over advancements in new or enhanced technology your competitors may start using. But you can upgrade your technology in time to turn this looming threat into a nonfactor.

Putting off the examination of potential Threats could be the most detrimental decision an organization could make. Identifying Threats and writing your Organization Threats Statement is the key to early detection that will result in the plans needed to address the Threats. As Jack Walsh, former President of General Electrics said, you must "face reality as it is, not as it was or as you wish it to be."

I'm not saying it's easy to win against a Threat. But you have no chance to win unless you first face reality and then prepare a plan to address it.

> *Don't be afraid of opposition. Remember, a kite*
> *rises against—not with—the wind.*

—**HAMILTON MABIE** (An American essayist who died in 1916).

New Threats to your organization can appear at any time. All organizations will, at some point, face challenges from changing marketplaces. Some of these challenges, at the most extreme level, will be Threats that can destroy your organization. Organizations that stay around do so with creativity, innovation and a commitment to adapting to constantly changing circumstances.

Typewriter manufacturers were once incredibly successful but later were rapidly eliminated by the computer. Kodak, which once dominated the film-development business, suffered greatly when digital cameras became the dominant mode of photography. Many manufacturers that long depended on nonrecyclable packaging did not visualize or adjust to the impact from green-thinking buyers.

Early awareness of Threats, followed by the development and execution of Organization Plans to address them, has meant the difference between some organizations surviving or disappearing.

Organization Threats

The following questions will help you identify potential Threats your organization may be facing. Remember to look at it with clear eyes rather than answering according to wishful thinking.

Technology

- Is there new Web-based competition?
- Is competition using more efficient or advanced technology?
- Are your managers aware of emerging technology trends in your industry?

Management and Other Personnel

- Does your organization have an essential manager with health problems?
- Is there a potential shortage of key non-management employees?

Financial Factors

- Will higher interest rates greatly impact your organization?
- Does your organization have principal-cost increases that are tied to cost-of-living increases? (Such as a union contract with raises tied to cost-of-living increases.)
- Will a drop in exchange rates raise your cost of raw materials purchased overseas?
- Could your organization lose any of its trade credit or borrowing loans?
- Does your organization have adequate corporate liability insurance?

Sales and marketing

- Are there trends that may negatively affect the nature of the competition you face, such as commodity sellers like Wal-Mart or other big-box stores?
- Is there a possibility of key suppliers beginning to compete directly?
- Are your sales too dependent on one customer?

Manufacturing, Operations and Distribution

- Is there a potential large increase in cost of materials used in production?
- Is there potential for a shortage of raw materials needed by your organization?
- Is your business an "easy-entry" business for new competitors?
- Are there technological changes on the horizon that your organization needs to accommodate or leverage?

Products/Services

- Is demand for your primary product/service decreasing?
- Are competitors underpricing your products because they have lower costs or more effective production methods?
- Is your organization exposed because new products have entered the market that make yours potentially obsolete?

KDM Related Threats

- Does your KDM have health issues?
- Are the partners who collectively own the organization out of alignment on key decisions, causing management to split into factions with each group supporting a different owner?

Organization Threats Relating to the KDM

Discussions concerning threats involving your KDM may be hard to bring up at the SLT SWOT meetings, but are very important to your organization's future. One KDM suffered two heart attacks within a short period of time. During his SLT's "SWOT" discussion, he identified his heart problem as a Threat that could significantly negatively affect his organization.

Written Organization Threats Statement

Creating your Organization Threats Statement is important for showing the need to develop an organization response that may prevent or minimize a serious problem. You want to have the maximum amount of time to prepare your organization to leap these hurdles if or when they appear.

Example Of An organization's Written Threats Statement

The following is an example of part of a written Organization Threats Statement:

- Competition alternatives are available online at lower prices than ours because they do not have to pay the high commission amount we pay our dealer network;
- Possible new Government regulations for manufacturing;
- Only nine years left on our patents.

Now Write Your Organization Threats Statement

When developing your written Organization Threats Statement, ask yourself which of your identified Threats are the biggest obstacles preventing your organization from attaining its Organization Vision Statement. These are the Threats that need to be in your formal written Organization Threats Statement.

You Are Now Ready For Creating Organization Critical Success Factors Statements

Once your team has completed your organization's written SWOT statements, you will be ready for the third step of your organization Organization Diagnostic: identifying the factors that are most critical to your organization's success.

CHAPTER 7

Organization Critical Success Factors

The third Step of your Organization Diagnostic is to complete an organization Critical Success Factors (CSFs) evaluation resulting in a written Organization CSF Statement. Critical Success Factors are those factors that are most critical to the success of your organization. Every organization is faced with factors that are critical to its success. The results of the first two steps of your organization diagnostic will be a great help to you in identifying your organization's CSFs. Many times, the SLT is too eager to move into action right away. They tend to develop important organization plans before taking the time to do the diagnostics needed to identify where their organization should be focusing resources before working on their organization plans.

By this point, I hope you see why it is so important to do your organization diagnostic, including this step of identifying your Critical Success Factors, before starting work on your written Organization Strategic Plans. Identifying CSFs will become extremely important in showing your SLT where the organization should best direct individual and collective employee time and energy, as well as financial resources.

Identifying your organization CSFs starts by you answering the question of what is "X" in, *"If X does not take place, the long-term dreams for the organization, as expressed in the Organization Vision Statement, will not be achieved."* Another way of expressing this is to ask, "What are the most impactful factors that could make my Organization Vision Statement happen?"

A CSF must only have the potential for high positive economic impact. To list a low impact factor could result in mistakenly misallocating organization resources by pursuing a CSF that, if achieved, will have too little impact on your organization.

Your Organization CSFs will be unique to your organization because they are directly related to your unique Organization Vision Statement. Keep your answers to the "X" question conceptual and without measurements, time lines or dollar amounts. Profit alone cannot be a CSF because profit is as much a part of a for-profit organization as the act of breathing is to your survival.

A CSF of one Organization identified "X" as follows: *"If we don't proactively address the weakness of needed and currently missing specialized talent in upper management, the Organization Vision will not be achieved."* Another organization identified a CSF of *"significantly reducing our manufacturing costs per unit so that we can price our products more competitively."*

Typical CSFs of other organizations involve short statements about such factors as the need for improved marketing, to develop a unique product, to create a formal sales process and to improve distribution efficiency.

Organization Critical Success Factors Relating To The KDM

The smaller the organization, the more likely that some of the most important factors critical to the success of the organization will be highly dependent on the efforts of the KDM. For example, one organization identified as an organization CSF the need for the KDM to spend more time on things that could have "Big Picture" impact upon the success of his organization, instead of spending most of his time doing things that an hourly employee could be doing.

Organization Vision Statement May Need To Be Reconsidered

Sometimes the answer to the X question may point you to the conclusion that your Organization Vision Statement may need to be reconsidered. There may be CSFs that are very real but are not realistically achievable. This may result in modifying your written Organization Vision Statement. Your organization may simply not have the capability to achieve the CSF. For example, you may identify a CSF to develop and sell a new product that may have the potential to generate great profits; but the CSF may be unachievable because it requires human or financial capabilities beyond your organization's current capacity.

Questions To Help You Identify Your Organization Critical Success Factors

The following questions will help you identify your organization's Critical Success Factors. While not all encompassing, these questions will help you uncover some of the most common CSFs for your organization.

- What new product, service or process requiring development does your organization need? *E.g. We need to compete more effectively; we need a low-priced entry-level product with fewer features.*
- What area of excellence or customer/client impact does your organization need? *E.g. We need to greatly improve Customer Loyalty.*
- What market area needs expansion? *E.g. We need to expand our market area so that we sell regionally rather than just locally.*
- What better use of capacity or efficiency is needed to reduce per unit cost? *E.g. We need to excel at increasing output from costly machinery.*
- What improved technology or know-how is needed? *E.g. We need newer high-tech equipment to get greater plant cost efficiency.*
- What improvements in your sales and marketing methods, practices or personnel are needed? *E.g. We need to improve our virtual/electronic marketing efforts, including social media.*

- What improvements in your distribution method or ordering system effectiveness are needed? *E.g. Our website must provide more efficient electronic ordering capabilities to our customers.*
- Are changes needed in the location or size of your headquarters or distribution plants? *E.g. We need to expand the number of units we have for sale by increasing the size of our distribution plant.*

Creating Your Written Organization CSF Statement

The time has come for your SLT to identify the CSFs for your organization and create your written Organization CSFs Statement. This is done by asking for and writing down suggested CSFs from each of your SLT members. After all the CSF suggestions are written down, each CSF needs to be challenged by other team members. Once you have done so, remove all but the five most critical CSFs, and these will be the CSFs that should be set forth as *the most* essential factors to your organization's success in your written Organization CSF Statement.

Driving CSF (DCSF)

You will be ready to start writing your first Organization Strategic Plan when you identify which of your CSFs is most needed for your organization to successfully excel or, in some cases, to survive. That CSF should be identified as your organization's DCSF, which I will sometimes refer to as your organization DCSF. Your DCSF holds the greatest economic importance for your organization. It will be the factor around which your first and most important Organization Strategic Plan will be built.

Selecting which of the factors in your Organization CSF Statement should be selected as your organization DCSF will require discussions among your SLT. You may find that this discussion brings about great differences of opinion among team members. But these discussions are essential. If there is not agreement among your SLT members, your KDM will make the final decision.

Your DCSF must have the potential to have a major positive impact on your organization. The DCSF for a manufacturing organization is an example of a factor with major impact. It was "To make greater use of expensive manufacturing equipment that is owned, but underutilized so that manufacturing can be done without increasing fixed equipment costs and, in turn, create greater profits."

CSFs May Change

Periodically certain impactful events take place that will require you to rethink and redefine your organization DCSFs.

Ready For Section Four – Strategic Plans

Once you have completed the three steps of your organization diagnostic, you will be ready to create plans and Key Performance Indicators (KPIs) that will make use of what you have discovered in doing the organization diagnostic.

SECTION 4

Strategic Plan Development

Organization plans conceived by your SLT, which I refer to as Organization Plans, come about during SLT meetings, during which your team focuses methodically, with patience and tenacity to create strategic plans. These Organization Plans will help your organization successfully face current and future obstacles with the best use of its resources.

If your organization is already successful, your Organization Plans will show you how to strategically grow your organization to the next level of success and avoid major problems due to rapid growth. If your organization is facing tough economic times, or is in sheer survival mode, the Organization Planning process will help your organization identify the essential changes needed to successfully fight through. Lack of well-conceived Organization Plans has resulted in many organizations not sticking around, because they were not able to weather major challenges that came their way.

Too many organizations move fences without clarity on where they need to be placed, in what way and by when. Organization Plans show where to move the fence, how to move it and by when, rather than reacting on the spur of the moment.

As with any journey, there are bound to be rough spots and even unexpected detours. But you will overcome these challenges if your SLT and all other employees have a high level of commitment to making your Organization Plans succeed. This commitment will help your organization move toward the vision for what the organization should look like five to ten years in the future, as reflected in the Organization Vision Statement. The quest to develop innovative plans that work, in spite of obstacles, is often not the easy or quick route. Creating and implementing good Organization Plans takes time, but the strategic changes from the process will power your organization's journey to achieve the future you desire.

Four Factors Required For Each Organization Plan

A single Organization Plan consists of the following components:

1. One Goal for each Organization Plan;
2. Up to five Strategies that conceptually show how you will achieve the Goal;
3. Up to five Action Plans for each Strategy that do what is needed for a specific Strategy to be effective;
4. An unlimited number of Tactics to carry out the Action Plans.

Responsibility For Creating Organization Plans

Your SLT is responsible for developing the Goal, Strategies and Action Plans of your Organization Plans. The SLT is also collectively responsible for achieving the desired results of the Organization Plans. However, a designated SLT member will be responsible for developing each Action Plan and the Tactics for the plan.

Limit Number of Organization Plans

One of the most common mistakes made by organizations is creating too many Organization Plans for their particular organization's infrastructure to handle. If your organization is working on too many

Organization Plans, it spreads your resources thin. When this happens, your organization may not accomplish the Goals of any of your Organization Plans.

The larger your organization, the better your organization can manage working on more than one Organization Plan. However, my experience has been that even large organiza-

A common factor in many underachieving organizations is that they focus on acting quickly rather than taking the time to plan how their organizations can have the best chance to attain the greatest amount of success.

tions with a lot of SLT time availability and financial resources should start with only one or two Organization Plans. Also, they will likely not succeed if more than five Organization Plans are being worked on simultaneously.

The flip side of the coin is that most small organizations are better served by focusing on developing only one or two Organization Plans at any time. This is because they typically do not have the available SLT time and other resources.

Regardless as to how many plans your organization develops, be sure there are sufficient resources for succeeding with your Organization Plans aimed at achieving your organization's DCSFs, before you put into effect any lesser important Organization Plans. In order to know this, the SLT ideally needs to develop at least a forecasted "ballpark" budget for accomplishing each Organization Plan.

Now, let's go into more detail on how to develop the Goals for each of your Organization Plans.

CHAPTER 8

Goals

Years ago, I had the opportunity to meet bestselling author Dr. Stephen Covey. We discussed many issues and found there were certain values we shared. One of them was the second habit expressed in his classic book, *The Seven Habits of Highly Effective People* (1989). Covey describes the second habit as "Beginning with the end in mind." Covey described this value as the key differentiation between successful organizations and those that didn't achieve their potential. The achieving organization, he noted, is much more likely to include an emphasis on management having a limited number of clear objectives, and employees understanding those few objectives and focusing most of their energies on them, so they could be attained.

This philosophy is integrated into the following required characteristics of each Goal:

Realistically Achievable

Goals must be realistically achievable. When the Goal is not realistically achievable, the result is counterproductive, causing poor focus

> *Unrealistic Goals are just a setup for your organization to fail, and these Goals will also damage respect for organization leaders who communicate the Goals.*

of employee energies on what needs to be done to accomplish the Goal. When the Goal is not realistically achievable, there is also a negative impact on employee respect for the organization's leadership—the communicators of the Goal.

Measurable

The Goals must be measurable and written in a clear, easy-to-understand way so your employees can periodically assess the effectiveness of the Goal. Ask questions to help identify the specific measurable of your Goals. For example, one KDM asked his fellow SLT members "What measurable target for customer satisfaction do we need to satisfy our Critical Success Factor of increase customer satisfaction?" The answer led to a Goal of "Get a minimum 80-percent satisfied rating from our customers within three years."

The question "What increase in sales is needed for each of our major product or service classifications?" led to a Goal of "Increase company sales threefold within three years through the use of independent sales representatives."

The question "How much does our operating cost need to be reduced for our primary product/service to be competitive?" led to the Goal of "Reduce average manufacturing cost per part by 20% within two years."

The question "Where are the best new markets for us to sell our products" led to the Goal of "Expand sales exports into six additional countries in the next 2 years."

The following are other examples of the type of questions that help develop Goals:

- What increase is needed in cash flow?
- What current asset-to-liability ratio and/or debt-to-equity ratio is needed to satisfy your bank loan agreement?

- What annual revenue do you need to meet a specific ranking in your industry?
- What does your organization need in measurable improved rates of repeat sales or retention of customers/clients?
- What is the needed rate (percentage) of sales increase from all products and services for the next three years?

Timelines

Goals must be achievable in a maximum of three years, although they may be reached much earlier. My experience has been that Goals that are several years or more into the future typically do *NOT* succeed because the nature of business requires more immediate results to maintain the focus of the KDM, SLT members and other company employees. I have seen many cases where goals longer than three years were never achieved because the SLT got sidetracked with shorter-term Goals that took no more than three years to achieve.

It is common for a Goal timeline to have benchmark dates for completion of *intermediate* steps that need to be satisfactorily completed while moving toward the full Goal. These *intermediate* benchmarks for a 30 percent increase by the end of the third year may be something such as a 10 percent increase in sales the first year and a 20 percent increase the second year. It is easy to see that these intermediate benchmark measurements allow you to determine whether the results are on course.

> *Make sure the Goal of each Organization Plan is clearly written with easy-to-understand measurements and timelines.*

Driving Organization Plan(s)

The Goal of one of your Organization Plans, typically the first plan, should, if successful, satisfy the factor that you have identified, during the diagnostic stage, as your organization's DCSF. Some organizations have two CSFs that, after discussion, are considered by the SLT to be of equal importance. If your organization has two equally Driving CSFs, your SLT should develop two different Organization Plans that each have a Goal addressing one of the two Driving CSFs. Identifying your most important Organization Plan, or two Organization Plans, is your first task.

Goals Often Capitalize on Opportunities

One company increased profits dramatically because of an Organization Plan that took advantage of an opportunity to use under-utilized manufacturing equipment and excess factory space. The company created and implemented an Organization Plan to double its production over a three-year period without having to invest in additional equipment or building space.

Some Potential Goals Have Too Much Risk

Think twice about developing a Goal to take advantage of an opportunity that excites you or may be unbearably tantalizing but has significant risk to the organization if the Goal is not achieved. For example, investing in a new facility and equipment for producing new products when you have no other use for the facility or equipment if the new products do not sell.

One KDM saw an Opportunity when the company was offered a contract with a national company that would result in an enormous increase in company sales with more than 50 percent of his revenue coming from just one customer—the national company. The purchasing agent of the customer told the KDM that the customer would be buying from them for many years if happy with the product.

The KDM proposed a Goal involving signing the contract and also borrowing a specific amount for the investment in equipment and personnel needed to fulfill the contract. His SLT didn't think they should take the Opportunity because they thought the company would be too dependent on the national-company customer. The CFO proposed the company not have more than 20 percent of annual sales volume tied to any one customer. His advice was to not move forward without a long-term written commitment from the prospective new customer.

The KDM said it was finally the company's chance at "big money" and ignored the SLT's warning. He forced an Organization Plan on the SLT with a Goal that included a greatly expanded processing plant and warehouse. The Goal required purchasing millions of dollars worth of sophisticated equipment to service the contract.

Not long after the building expansion was complete and the new equipment installed, the customer switched to another supplier. The company was left with excess capacity and higher fixed costs, greatly hurting the company financially.

Most successful business leaders have, at some time, taken assertive moves to advance their organizations by setting a Goal that takes advantage of an Opportunity. In order to grab hold of the Opportunity, they needed bold Goals with Action Plans that involved calculated risks. Taking calculated risks is different from gambling. But you have to carefully consider the negative impact if the plan fails to achieve the Goal.

Organization Resources Not Sufficient To Capitalize On Opportunity

Some Opportunities sound great, and are great, but are just not realistically attainable or practical for your organization because your organization lacks the resources to take advantage of the opportunity. **No organization has the infrastructure and capital to tackle and achieve every Opportunity.** For example, creating a Goal to take advantage of a new Opportunity that requires adding new employees, or training current employees in new skills, at a time your organization is not in a position to shift financial resources because they are needed elsewhere is not realistically achievable.

Your SLT needs to determine if setting a Goal to take advantage of an Opportunity is worth diverting your organization's available human and financial resources away from where they are currently being utilized.

One KDM was excited about opening a new plant to produce

certain parts her company used, rather than contracting for them with a supplier. She believed her company could save significant money by manufacturing these parts for her company and others. She explained to her SLT her belief that her company would be able to use about 20% of the parts produced and the cost savings from making the parts would be significant.

At a SLT meeting, her Operations Manager pointed out the company did not have sufficient expertise with manufacturing these parts. He questioned whether the company could control the quality or costs of manufacturing the parts. The company CFO expressed her concern that producing the parts would divert financial and human resources from present commitments relating to the Organization Plan, and a Goal addressing the company's DCSF, on which the company was focusing. The Opportunity was real, but the SLT made the wise decision to pass on it.

Organization Plans With Goals Preparing For Threats

Many organizations face Threats that lead to Goals for neutralizing these Threats. However, these Goals may still not be achievable depending upon the nature of the Threat. For example, if your organization faces a Threat from web-based competition, you cannot eliminate the new competition. Instead, you need to ask "How am I going to react to it?"

One company's sales were represented by a small number of major accounts. The potential negative impact if a couple of these companies quit as accounts was identified during the organization SWOT as a significant Threat to the company. This Threat became the basis for a Critical Success Factor of "decrease our dependence on the small number of customers that represent most of the company sales so that we would not be significantly financially hurt if we lost one or even a few of these major accounts." The Goal of the first Organization Plan developed by the company was "do what is needed to bring about a situation where no one account customer accounts for over 20 percent of the company's projected gross annual revenue/turnover."

One manufacturing company, which had been successful for several decades selling its products via paper catalogues, started to face new competition when the Internet created the ability for companies to offer lower pricing for similar products because of not having the substantial cost of creating, producing and shipping catalogues.

The Threat couldn't be eliminated, but early awareness of the Threat resulted in the company reacting in time to avoid a catastrophe. An Organization Plan was created with a goal of offering their entire inventory via the web in six months. The plan required several different departments to have Action Plans for their part in this major course change. As a result of executing the plan, the company is able to compete effectively with their web-based competition.

Organization Plan Mostly Involving The Department Of One SLT Member

One of the most common mistakes in strategic planning is the creation of an Organization Plan that is totally or almost totally the responsibility of one SLT member. In most cases where only one SLT member is responsible for achieving this plan, the plan should be treated as an Action Plan (discussed in detail later in this section) for that SLT member's department. The Action Plan objective may be discussed by the SLT but the assigned SLT member is largely responsible for its success.

Give strong consideration as to whether your team is treating a plan as an Organization Plan that would be best treated as an Action Plan with an objective that is only one piece of a much larger Organization Plan. The Director of Sales asked for a special SLT meeting with a request that the team develop an Organization Plan with a Goal to address sales people leaving and taking key accounts with them. The Threat of losing sales employees who go on to compete in some manner cannot be fully controlled. But there may be things that can be done to neutralize the negative impact of the salespeople leaving and taking key accounts.

The team met and decided that the needed plan would be an Action Plan for which the Director of Sales would be responsible. One of the

SLT members recommended the Action Plan include a strategy of splitting up key accounts to keep any one salesperson from having too many exclusive relationships with the company's large key accounts.

One of the other SLT members suggested a strategy of giving new financial incentives to the sales staff in return for having the company salespeople sign non–compete agreements as part consideration for getting new financial incentives, prohibiting them from competing for the company accounts for one year from when they were no longer with the company. This company operated in an area where such non-compete agreements were legal and enforceable, and the Action Plan resulted in creating and executing such agreements with the sales staff.

Another example involved a SLT member's concern that those reporting to her did not have a strong technology background. She realized they would be able to contribute more to her department's results if they improved their technical abilities. She brought this up to the SLT. They didn't see this as a Goal of an Organization Plan. They suggested she develop an Action Plan, which, among other things, gave a financial incentive to the employees who took certain technology courses.

CHAPTER 9

Organization Plan Strategies

Your next step is to identify the Strategies needed to achieve each Goal. Strategies are the conceptual guidance system that brings you to completion of your Goals. For every Goal, you need to develop a Strategy or Strategies for achieving the Goal. Each Strategy must clearly lead to your Goal.

The number of Strategies you develop for each Goal will be dependent upon your organization's ability to effectively execute the Strategies' Action Plans, but no Goal should have more than five Strategies. As you will see later, each of the Strategies is required to have Action Plans.

Strategies must be conceptual, not measurable, detailed or specific. An example of the conceptual nature of a Strategy would be "Leverage our unique manufacturing process to attain our Goal of increased market share."

There is no one person who is responsible for the success of a Strategy because success for each strategy will be driven by Action Plans, which will each have a Responsible Party. (I will discuss Action Plans in the next Chapter.)

Creative Thinking

Creating Strategies is, in many ways, an art. So approach the development of Strategies with the maximum amount of creativity. This kind of creativity is based on past experience and specialized knowledge of your organization, your industry and your leading competitors. All of these help create Strategies, but instinct and intuition also play an important role in developing "out of the box" Strategies. This type of creative thinking can only occur when you remain open to breaking the status quo, and it comes from those who are not locked into the common thinking of their industry.

Change is not comfortable for many, but it is important to strive to develop creative Strategies. Be prepared for resistance from others who might respond to new Strategy ideas negatively or by invoking the popular adage "If it ain't broke, don't fix it." This kind of thinking has resulted in keeping many organizations from developing Strategies that would have moved them from good to great.

Jeff Bezos, the Founder and CEO of Amazon, gave a TV interview during which he discussed his view regarding the need for an organization to be constantly adapting or, if they fail to, go out of business. One of the key points Bezos made was that we could complain about the market dictating the need to change and innovate, but complaining isn't a Strategy. In fact, in a direct quote in response to a question about Amazon putting bookstores out of business, he said, "Amazon isn't happening to bookselling; the future is happening to bookselling."

Creating successful Strategies requires that your SLT proactively look for and find innovative ways to overcome the challenges, rather than using the challenges as reasons for inertia. Ideally, your SLT will be open-minded towards innovative approaches and embrace tests that try new ways of doing things and adaptations/variations of old ways of doing things.

You Do Not Need To Be 100% Sure That A Strategy Will Succeed

You do not need to be 100% sure that a Strategy will succeed before you make the decision to try a Strategy. You may be making the right decision by creating a Strategy even if the Strategy doesn't work. It's easy to find reasons why you shouldn't try a Strategy or give reasons why some Strategy cannot work. High-impact leaders, on the other hand, try innovative Strategies that might

> *When an organization's leadership team is seen as embracing Strategies, it sets an example for all others in the organization to be innovative.*

make things work. They look at the potential upside of a new Strategy working compared to the downside of not trying the Strategy.

Consider Your Organization SWOT When Creating Strategies

The organization evaluation information disclosed in your Organization SWOT, as explained in Section 2, will help you create Strategies for your Goals. Your Organization SWOT will point out what best utilizes your organization Strengths, neutralizes Weaknesses, takes advantage of Opportunities and prepares you as best as possible for addressing Threats outside your control.

The best Strategies to achieve Goals often involve making greater use of the areas in which your organization has Strengths. Is there a strength identified in your organization Strengths Statement that, if used to a much greater degree, could be helpful to your organization's efforts in reaching a goal?

Take note of your organization Weaknesses, especially those that exist to a greater degree in your organization than they do for your competitors. Ask yourself whether you need Strategies to neutralize these Weaknesses in order for your Organization Goals to succeed. The last thing you want to do is try to beat your competition in a business area that requires a skill or other factor that is a Weakness for your organization but a Strength of your competitor. Watch out for proposed Strategies that require capabilities outside of your organization resources.

Is there an Opportunity identified in your Organization Opportunities Statement that can be important to a Strategy to help achieve one of your Goals?

One company developed an Organization Plan with the goal of doubling the company's production of its primary product within three years while reducing the manufacturing cost per unit by 15 percent by year three. One Strategy identified was to take advantage of the Opportunity to "better utilize the company's existing, underutilized building and equipment." There were, of course, other Strategies, such as increasing company sales by the engagement of independent sales representatives in areas in which the company sales staff did not already operate. The Strategies worked, and the Goal was achieved.

Is there a Threat you identified in your Organization Threats Statement, which, if not addressed or prepared for by your organization, can derail the chances of your organization's Strategies bringing about the success of an Organization Goal? Look realistically at what Strategy can be developed to neutralize a Threat so that it does not stop your Goal from being achieved.

Below are examples of Strategies developed by other organizations:

Strategy Examples

- Use the common characteristics of the geographic markets in which we are currently successful to identify other geographic markets for further expansion.
- Improve our organization's marketing efforts to get needed clients for our desired growth.
- Create a market niche that differentiates our services from our competitors.
- Change our pricing strategy to one more competitive with the market.
- Increase our compensation programs to motivate salespeople to sell more of our high-gross-profit products.
- Hire a full-time sales manager with successful sales management and training experience to increase sales staff results.
- Survey customers who have stopped buying from us to find ways to increase customer retention.
- Develop additional products to sell to current customers.

- Create financial incentives to increase referrals from our satisfied customers.
- Provide our sales force with better prospect management tools.
- Stop producing our unsuccessful products.
- Add features to our products that would create greater value for our products compared to our competition.
- Improve organization culture by cutting down on organization bureaucracy and minimizing organization politics.
- Improve organization communications between departments from bottom to top.
- Improve our infrastructure by adding a Director of Human Resources.
- Improve our Web technology and functions.
- Engage a professional to improve employee relations.
- Dismiss our poorest performing employees.
- Offer to pay for online training courses for our employees that would facilitate their professional growth in ways that lead to organization results improvement.

Before you finalize your Strategies, stop and ask yourself, "If my organization achieves these Strategies, will the Goal be accomplished?"

CHAPTER 10

Action Plans For Each Strategy

After you create a Strategy, you need to create Action Plans to show what needs to be done to accomplish each Strategy. You can have up to five Action Plans for each Strategy. Each of the Action Plans must meet the SMART criteria. The SMART criterion require the Action Plan be Specific, Measurable, Achievable, have a SLT member who is Responsible for the results of the Action Plan and that the Action Plan must be completed within certain Time frames.

It is important to note that Action *Plans* are not Action *Items*. Action Plans are plans themselves and can be quite complex with many steps. An Action Plan could be to develop a new website for a brand new product. The Action Plan in turn consists of multiple Tactics which are the individual tasks that need to be accomplished in order to achieve the Action Plan.

Let's take a closer look at each of the **SMART** criteria:

(S) Specific:

It must be very clear as to what is expected to take place within the deadline. For example, a commitment to having a certain project "mostly ready sometime next week" is not as specific as a commitment that the project will be "ready to send to customer X no later than 9:00 am Wednesday."

There also needs to be clarity as to what it means by 'getting something done'. With some, this means getting it done perfectly. With others, it means getting it done in a way that honors time commitments, but without waiting until everything is perfect. Spell out exactly what needs to be done, step by important step. If written sufficiently specific, there should be no ambiguity as to whether an Action Plan is completed or not.

The SLT Responsible Party is also responsible for identifying the specific tactics (more about Tactics in the next chapter) needed to execute the Action Plan and the specific resource needs such as funding, staffing and building/equipment.

(M) Measurable

You must know upfront how results from your Action Plans will be measured, and these measurements must be clear and objective. This is the only way you will know whether or not you are on target. There are different methods for measuring results, such as increasing sales by a certain percentage or revenue amount.

(A) Achievable

Your Action Plan must have a realistic chance of success; otherwise, the Action Plan will be demoralizing to the Responsible Party and all other employees working on the Action Plan.

(R) Responsible Party

A specific person, referred to as the Responsible Party, is responsible and committed to achieving the result of each Action Plan. Each Action Plan must identify one person, and only one, who is the point person responsible for driving a specific Action Plan to success. This responsibility also includes coming up with the different Tactics needed to make the Action Plan succeed and giving updates on the status of the Action Plan to the SLT at SLT meetings.

The Responsible Party must have the authority, as well as the responsibility, to see it through to success. This authority includes assigning tasks needed to implement the Action Plan. Most Responsible Parties are assigned responsibility for creating and implementing Action Plans that exclusively involve the department or business functions that report to them. Consequently, most Tactics for the Action Plan are assigned to employees working for the Responsible Party. There may be times, however, when, with the approval of other managers, the Responsible Party may need help from employees who report to other managers.

(T) Time Frame

Action Plans need deadlines. A realistic Time Frame must be established and agreed to between the Responsible Party and the SLT for when an Action Plan is to be successfully completed. Many Action Plans also include the outside date for when each part or milestone of the Action Plan are to be completed.

Deadlines for Action Plans are sometimes suggested by the KDM or by other SLT members, but it is important the Responsible Party for the Action Plan deadline not commit to the final deadline until the Tactics for the Action Plan are specified. That is, I recommend taking a "bottom up" approach for determining timeframes. Typically, the date first established for completing an Action Plan is understood to not be a final date until the Responsible Party identifies the Tactics needed to accomplish the Action Plan. In addition, the Responsible Party needs to have a realistic idea about the ability of others to accomplish the specific Tactics within the allotted timeframe.

If a Responsible Party feels strongly that an Action Plan is not likely to be completed by the requested time, it is important to not give a "commitment" to the requested deadline.

Sometimes conflicts arise because of

the Responsible Party's inability or unwillingness to push back against an unrealistic deadline proposed by the KDM or other members of the SLT. But that ability to push back—tactfully of course—is essential when a deadline request does not intersect with the reality of the working world. The final timeline agreed to, unless there is a true crisis involved, should include a "cushion" period to allow for unexpected occurrences.

SLT Questions To Help Create Action Plans

The following are some of the questions asked by the SLT to help the Responsible Party, who in this example is the Sales Manager, create an Action Plan for a Strategy that included "adding additional salespeople to the sales staff," that was developed to achieve a Goal of "increasing company sales by 20 percent during year one of the Organization Plan."

- How many new salespeople will need to be hired this year to achieve the sales-increase Goal of 20 percent during year one?
- What tools (such as behavioral surveys and credit checks) should be used during the interviewing process for new sales employees in order to identify those likely to become good performing salespeople?
- What are the sales amounts we need new salespeople to generate, and how often will the Sales Manager review sales results?
- How much of the budget will be needed to hire, train and compensate the new salespeople during the first 12 months of the Action Plan?

Organization SWOT Results Impact Action Plans

Action Plans, whether or not they are created to support an Organization Plan, should take advantage of certain organization Strengths, neutralize Weaknesses, take advantage of Opportunities and try to overcome Threats.

Limit Number of Action Plans for Each Strategy

Consider the amount of resources needed to successfully achieve 25 Action Plans if you have five strategies for one of your Organization Plans and five Action Plans for each strategy. Consequently, even a large organization should have no more than five Action Plans for each Strategy. The smaller your organization, the fewer Action Plans you should have for each Strategy. A small organization may only be able to effectively handle a couple of Action Plans.

A Strategy with too many Action Plans creates a situation that is not manageable, and the result is that none of the Action Plans get handled well and the Strategy does not happen.

If you believe one of your Strategies requires more than five Action Plans, then the Strategy is too complex. Break the Strategy into two or more separate Strategies. By doing this, you should always be able to keep a limit of no more than five Action Plans per Strategy.

One of the techniques for identifying necessary Action Plans involves your SLT brainstorming to come up with questions that prompt answers that reveal the type of Action Plans needed for different Strategies. The following are examples of the type of questions that can lead to great Action Plans related to improving your product line:

- What kind of Action Plan is needed to differentiate your organization's primary products or services from those of your competition?
- What kind of Action Plan is needed to lower the risk of product failure, as well as your cost of returned products?
- What kind of Action Plan is needed to improve your product in any of the following: appearance, installation cost and/or ease, price, ease of use, versatility, user and/or maintenance cost, durability, speed, size, material quality, and accuracy?
- What kind of Action Plan is needed to lower your prices based on improved internal efficiency?
- What kind of Action Plan is needed to lower costs, such as delivery, installation or financing?

- What kind of Action Plan is needed to process orders faster?
- What kind of Action Plan is needed to lower labor costs?

Action Plans Do Not Need To Be Connected To Organization Plans

In this Chapter, I have focused on Action Plans that address Strategies that are part of Organization Plans. But in the day-to-day running of an organization, Action Plans need to be developed and executed by managers at all levels—such Action Plans are in addition to any Action Plans that relate to Organization Plans. The Action-Plan guidelines discussed in this chapter also apply to the many Action Plans every organization manager is creating and implementing as part of their responsibility, whether or not connected to a Strategy in an Organization Plan.

If your Marketing Director decides a new marketing brochure aimed at certain potential clients is needed, the Marketing Director may develop an Action Plan for creation of the brochure, whether or not this Action Plan is part of an Organization Plan. This is an example of the type of things that come up and need to be addressed routinely in business. It is not going to show up on the Organization Plan which is more strategic in nature. However, these types of plans are a normal course of business and will need Action Plans for them as well.

It Is Time To Look At Tactics

In the next chapter, we look at the Tactics needed to carryout the Action Plans.

CHAPTER 11

Action Plan Tactics

Tactics are the individual tasks that get results for Action Plans. For example, if the Action Plan is to build a website, Tactics will include finding a developer, building the site content and testing the site before it goes live. The Responsible Party for an Action Plan is responsible for identifying the Tactics needed to make the Action Plan successful, assigning the Tactics to a Responsible Party and monitoring the results.

Once a SLT member has been designated as the Responsible Party for an Action Plan, he or she can *immediately* start to develop Tactics. The Responsible Party for the Action Plan may request help from subordinate departments, teams, or selected other managers for developing Tactics. It takes a lot of effort to create good Tactics. The Responsible Party should not make the mistake of not putting in the same level of energy and focus on developing Tactics as was spent by the SLT in creating the other elements of the Organization Plans.

When the Responsible Party has identified the Tactics to be used in an Action Plan, it is common for the Responsible Party to inform the SLT, at a meeting of the SLT, of at least an overview of some, or all, of the Tactics without going into details as to who will be carrying out which Tactic. The SLT, as a group, does not create the Tactics. SLT members may discuss their thoughts about the Tactics for the Action Plan and even offer suggestions for additional Tactics.

No Limit To The Number Of Tactics

Tactics break down what may seem to be an overwhelming Action Plan objective into small, manageable units. There is no limit to the number of Tactics you can use to carry out each Action Plan, other than the practical constraints of your organization's infrastructure and resources to be able to complete the Tactics in a timely manner. It is typical to need many Tactics for each Action Plan.

> *The SLT, as a group, is typically not deeply involved in developing or monitoring Tactics.*

Tying It Together

Remember the company I mentioned in Section Three where the KDM identified company marketing as a company Strength, and a SLT member pointed out how the company's marketing results were actually weak based upon industry comparatives? After a lot of discussion, the KDM agreed with the other members of the SLT that an Organization Plan was needed that would get company marketing results up to at least the industry average within two years.

One of the Strategies identified involved evaluating and changing the marketing team staff. One of the Action Plans, which had one of the SLT members as the Responsible Party, was to hire a new Director of Marketing by a specific date. The Tactics in the Action Plan for making this happen included a Tactic of developing a compensation program to attract candidates for the job. There was a Tactic for identifying the best methods of recruiting for the position and a Tactic for tools used and background checks needed in selecting the right person. These Tactics were identified by the Responsible Party, who shared the Tactics with other members of the SLT.

Consider Questions That Will Help You Write Tactics

The following questions were used to help a Sales Manger identify the Tactics for hiring two new salespeople:

- Who will create (or update) a job description for the salespeople, and by what date must it be completed?
- How will the salespeople be recruited?
- How will the salespeople be compensated?
- Who will conduct the interviews?
- What selection criteria will be used?
- By what date must the salespeople be hired and start employment?
- By what dates must the salespeople start and complete training?
- On what skills or product information will the salespeople need to be trained, and who will do the training?
- Who will create the training programs, and when is the deadline?
- What minimum sales results are expected from each salesperson and within what timeframe?

Assigning Tactics

After the Tactics are identified, the Responsible Party may elect to carry out some or all of the Tactics or may decide to assign the Tactics to someone else. The Responsible Party may assign the Tactics to different employees, teams or departments.

An example would be an Action Plan that calls for replacing a certain employee who is hurting the company culture because of his passive-aggressive style. The Responsible Party may assign to one employee one task of the Action Plan that involves firing, before the end of the month, the employee. The Tactic in the Action Plan of recruiting and hiring a replacement for the fired employee, with a 60-day deadline for doing so, might be assigned to another employee.

Assignments must be clearly understood by the employee(s) assigned to do the Tactics. This is best accomplished if the assignments are in writing and are specific and measurable.

Every Tactic assigned must have a deadline. Deadlines are likely to be relatively short-term. It is not uncommon for tactical commitments to have no longer than 30-day deadlines.

Example Of Tactics Spreadsheet For Technology Company

Let's look at the assigned Tactics for certain Action Plans of a technologies company:

Action Plans–Dave is Responsible Party	Tactics	Responsible Person(s)	Due Date
1. Expand the number of onsite training days to six and create twenty-four online training programs to allow more time for interactive training.	1. Develop PowerPoint and other materials for all training sessions. 2. Practice training support sessions before using with a training class. 3. Create short videos and other visuals to be embedded in Power-Point. 4. Move selected PowerPoint presentations into online training modules with exams.	1. Dave 2. Dave 3. Dave 4. Sharon	1. April 29 2. May 7 3. Sept 6 4. October 31
2. Create Survey by June 30th to be completed by trainees after each session to measure training effectiveness and satisfaction of trainees	1. Create survey questions.	1. Claire	1. May 7
3. Create pre-training materials by June 1st that need to be studied by trainees in advance of initial training, along with online open-book test.	1. Slides, handouts and case study materials to be created to train new facilitator/coaches on how to use with clients.	1. Claire	1. Before May Training.

Meet Regularly With The Parties Assigned To Do The Tasks

Each Responsible Party needs to meet regularly with the parties he or she has assigned to do the Tactics tasks. The Responsible Party needs these meetings to see how the Tactics are tracking and verify the Tactic dates are likely to be met.

CHAPTER 12

SLT Meetings to Create New Plans

Now that you understand what needs to be included in an Organization Plan and what isn't, let's look at the three different types of SLT meetings that are focused primarily on creating new Organization Plans.

The first type of meeting is the Organization Plan Development Workshop, scheduled specifically for creating your first organization plan or plans. The second is a Special SLT Planning Meeting that may be needed because an Organization Plan has been achieved or to respond to a significant change that has taken place. The third is a SLT Annual Organizational Planning Retreat, which is focused on refreshing the diagnostic efforts, but which may include developing a new Organization Plan because of what is pointed out from reviewing the diagnostic information.

Organization Plan Development Workshop

When you are ready to start creating Organization Plans, your first step is to schedule a time for a retreat or workshop called the Organization Plan Development Workshop. Your first Organization Plan, or Plans, will be created during this retreat or workshop. For retreats, some KDMs schedule only one day to start this process and if the organization needs additional time, a second full-day retreat meeting is scheduled to take place as soon as possible after the first retreat meeting day.

The Organization Plan Development Workshop starts with a review of answers from SLT members to both your Organization Diagnostic Questionnaire and the SWOT questions. Typically, the KDM will know the answers to these questions but the SLT will see only collective summaries of the answers, without knowing which answer came from which SLT member. The information is shared this way to avoid negative situations arising out of SLT members being offended by another member's opinion of them or their areas of responsibility.

After reviewing this information, the SLT works on developing written Organization SWOT Statements and written Organization Critical Success Factors. These two statements must be completed before the SLT considers creating the Goal for the first Organization Plan. The SLT may consider many different potential Goals but is limited to a maximum of two driving Goals, although having only one driving Goal is preferable.

After the Goal or Goals are established, the rest of the meeting will be spent getting Strategies for the Goal(s) and Action Plan(s) for each Strategy.

Special SLT Planning Meetings

Changed Circumstances Force Changed Organization Focus

Another time such meetings are scheduled is when circumstances have changed in a way that calls into question the focus of the organization, and the time sensitivity may be such that your organization should not delay addressing it until a scheduled SLT annual retreat meeting. Examples of this would be such things as when there is major new or changed competition, natural disasters or the loss of the organization's major client. For example, your organization may need an Organization Plan for a strategic reaction to a new Threat that has potential for significant negative impact on your organization.

Changed circumstances prompting Special SLT Meetings often involve factors an organization had not been faced with when your SLT created your last Organization Critical Success Factor. An SLT member typically requests a Special SLT Meeting the moment he/she becomes aware of a critical change.

For example, a Special SLT Meeting was called by the KDM of a software technology company to minimize the impact of the major accounts the company's former Sales Manager was trying to move to the company's biggest competitor. The Sales Manager had been with the KDM's company for over a decade. He not only managed the sales staff, he also generated most of the company's large account sales. By the time the Special SLT Meeting took place, two weeks after the Sales Manager left, he had already started contacting the large accounts he had worked with to move them over as clients of the new company.

It's easy to see why it was important enough for the SLT to call a Special SLT Meeting to create an Organization Plan to address the situation. The Organization Plan developed included a few different Strategies with some of the following Action Plans:

- The KDM personally handling the sales management and major account responsibilities in the interim until a new Sales Manager was hired and demonstrated ability to keep and add major clients.
- The Director of Human Resources searching for a new person to manage the sales force. None of the company sales staff were viewed as qualified to fill the Sales Manger's role.
- The CFO engaging an attorney to prepare templates for non-compete agreements that might prevent employees from competing for a reasonable period of time in the event they did leave the company.

Sometimes An Opportunity Develops That Wasn't Previously Available

Sometimes an Opportunity develops that wasn't previously available and your organization will need to react quickly or lose the Opportunity. Taking advantage of these Opportunities may be more important, time wise, than achieving the Goal of one of your current Organization Plan(s).

For example, the owner of a small contracting company decided to retire and sell his business. This was viewed by a larger company as an unexpected Opportunity for buying the assets and clients of the smaller company. An Organization Plan, on which the larger organization had been focusing, was moved down in priority during the Special SLT Meeting.

Another example of the type of things that result in the scheduling of a Special SLT Meeting is when a new product is rolled out by your existing competition and the product is totally new or better than your product. This might bring about a Special SLT Meeting to discuss whether your organization should develop an Organization Plan to develop products to compete with your competitor's new products.

Situations That Require A Major Reallocation Of Resources

A special meeting may be needed to discuss whether a major reallocation of resources from existing Organization Plans to a different purpose should take place.

A company's manufacturing plant, located in a 100-year flood plain area, experienced a historic flood. Water entered their building, rising several feet, making operations impossible. Some equipment was not working after the water subsided. The company was essentially shut down because of the natural disaster.

The KDM called a Special Meeting of the SLT. He requested the Operations VP prepare an analysis to show the SLT at the meeting to help them make a decision on whether to move the company equipment to a new location or to wait for the current location to dry out enough for the company to begin manufacturing again.

It is easy to see how this flood-related problem took priority over the current Organization Plans. They needed a plan that would consider things such as shifts in handling personnel matters, communications with customers who were waiting for their products and more things affected by the situation. At the Special Meeting, the SLT agreed that a new plan had to be created within 15 days, which was amazingly fast for such important decisions.

In another situation, a landlord surprised a construction company when it notified the company it would not renew the company's lease on the building. That day, a Special Meeting was called, even though the lease had six months to run. The SLT decided to not look for a new place to lease, but instead to create an Organization Plan for buying a new building. They agreed this plan would take priority over the existing Organization Plans because they needed to move in within less than six months.

SLT members had to divert significant time to this plan and had to drop working on other Organization Plans. For example, the Operations Manager became the Responsible Party for an Action Plan of finding a building that met certain criteria, including cost, size, location, etc. He was also made the Responsible Party for the Action Plan for moving the company equipment to the new facility when purchased. The company CFO was made the Responsible Party for creating a cash flow projection that showed the money the company would have to reallocate from other purposes for financing the purchase of a new building.

Organization Plan Has Been Achieved

There is a good occasion for having a Special SLT Planning Meeting. That is when an Organization Plan has been satisfactorily completed. A Special SLT Planning Meeting is generally called to develop a replacement Organization Plan. You don't want to wait for an annual meeting to come up with a replacement plan.

Organization Planning Retreat

At least two weeks before your Organization Planning Retreat, your KDM should ask each of the SLT members to submit their written responses to the Diagnostic Questionnaire that was discussed in Section Three. They need to also share their views in writing about each of the Organization's SWOT factors. The KDM should explain and give assurance that the KDM will not reveal to the SLT what any one SLT member responded to the Questionnaire and the SWOT. This is necessary to facilitate openness and sharing of opinions about things that may reflect poorly on a SLT member or the department of the member.

Before each Organization Planning Retreat Meeting, the KDM will create a summary of the SLT Diagnostic Questionnaire answers and SWOT Statements views. The summary of responses is handed out to SLT members at the beginning of the meeting for discussion. The handouts include no identification of who submitted any particular answers or responses.

At the beginning of your annual retreat meeting, the KDM, if the KDM is the facilitator, or your outside facilitator, should explain what you hope to accomplish at the retreat meeting and briefly go over the agenda for the meeting. The agenda for each Organization Planning Retreat Meeting should include an early-in-the-meeting review and discussion by the team of the summary of SLT Diagnostic Questionnaire answers as well as the summary of the SWOT responses.

After these discussions, a new Critical Success Factor Statement will be created based on facts known as of the time of the annual retreat meeting. These CSF Statements are based on all of the information that is known at the present time. The CSFs identified are often very different from those identified in the previous Organization Planning Retreat Meeting.

If, after the diagnostic discussions and creation of an organization Critical Success Factor Statement, it appears a new Organization Plan or Plans needs to be developed, the team should continue the retreat meeting, focusing on creating the new plan.

A new Critical Success Factor Statement is created during the team meeting after the Diagnostic questionnaire and SWOT discussions.

In some cases, the CSFs will involve major changes of things for which the SLT members may have been aware but did not have enough information to ascertain when their potential impact would become critical enough to warrant calling a Special SLT meeting.

At the Organization Planning Retreat, your team will NOT be monitoring the Strategies or Action Plans of your current Organization Plans since this is being done monthly. Tactics are also not to be discussed at these meetings.

Organization Planning Retreat Help Organizations Improve How They do Things

One of the benefits of the Organization Planning Retreat Meeting is that it helps keep organizations from continuing to do things the same way they have always done them. Let me share an example.

At the First Organization Plan Development Workshop of one manufacturing company, which I will refer to as Domestic Company, the SLT determined the Driving CSF to be new competition the company faced when their major competitor switched from manufacturing its products domestically to manufacturing in China. The competitor was able to significantly drop its prices because it had much lower wage costs with no decrease in product quality.

The SLT of Domestic Company looked at ways the company could keep its then-current prices but offer customers something extra that their competition did not provide. They could not find such ways. The SLT decided the potential impact of changed circumstances did not warrant a change of the company's basic business model to stay competitive.

But the SLT decided the new competitive factor did warrant a change in pricing philosophy. The Organization Plan developed at the first Organization Plan Development Workshop involved competing by lowering prices without changing any key areas of their organization's business model.

The positive was that the reduced level of sales that started with the competitor's announcement of the switch to manufacturing in China stopped when Domestic matched the dramatically lower prices on all its non-customized products that involved large manufacturing runs.

The negative was that lowering prices only delayed the impact of the new competition. It was turning out to be a formula for disaster. Domestic's lowered prices on its non-customized metal fabrication products resulted in a significant reduction of Domestic's gross profits leading to a major reduction of net profits.

At Domestic Company's Organizational Planning Retreat, the SLT focused on the challenge of the reduced gross and net profits of the company. Doing something about this was identified by the SLT as the DCSF. At the retreat, Domestic's SLT developed a new Organization Plan that involved focusing the company's sales efforts on customers needing time-sensitive metal fabricated products that were not as price sensitive because the customers were more concerned with getting them fast, rather than at the cheapest price. This strategy took advantage of the fact that the competitor's products took much longer to get to consumers because they were manufactured in China.

Location

Holding the Organization Planning Retreat away from the office minimizes the all-too-common interruptions that keep your SLT from strategic thinking. Organization Planning Retreat should be held in a location where there are very few distractions.

During your annual retreat time, your SLT should be able to step back from the activities on which they are working week in and week out and focus on strategic matters. During these Annual Retreat Meetings your SLT needs to pull back from their day-to-day efforts of putting out fires and focus strategically on the purposes of the meeting.

SLT Preparation for Annual Retreat

Before each annual retreat meeting, each SLT member must spend some time on pre-meeting preparation. This includes writing down thoughts on whether conditions have arisen that would warrant a greater degree of organization focus on a new Organization Plan over one or more of your current Organization Plans.

Manage With KPIs

Before we look at how your organization should execute your Organization Plans to get the best results, we need to look at how to identify the Key Performance Indicators, mentioned earlier in this chapter, that your SLT needs to monitor in order to manage properly.

SECTION 5

Key Performance Indicators (KPIs)

t's true — you cannot manage what you cannot measure! Key Performance Indicators (KPIs) are metrics that provide what you need to manage your organization. They provide a quantitative measurement of your organization's performance over time. KPIs are those measurable statistics that need to be monitored on a regular basis so there are no surprises. They should act as a "flash" report, giving you a quick understanding of how your organization is progressing, or can be expected to perform in the near future.

There are no "standard" KPIs that apply to every organization. Every organization has different driving forces, so KPIs will vary from one organization to another. Your organization needs to identify the KPIs that are essential to its success. Your SLT must review these on a regular basis, whether or not they become part of any Organization Plan or Action Plan. Monitoring these KPIs will give your SLT the warning time needed to make corrections, if required, before it is too late.

A Key Performance Indicator is a quantifiable measurement that reflects the following:

133

- **Key:** Information relating to a component that is important to success or failure
- **Performance:** Information about something that is capable of being influenced by individual behaviors or decisions
- **Indicator:** Information that indicates expected future performance

CHAPTER 13

Identifying KPIs to Monitor

In this Chapter, you will learn how to identify the KPIs your organization SLT needs to regularly monitor and determine how frequently the monitoring needs to occur.

KPI Selection Suggestions

The first step in identifying the KPIs your SLT needs to be regularly monitoring is for a KPI Workshop to be scheduled. A SLT meeting should be scheduled for a two-hour block of time to discuss and identify the relevant KPIs.

Your KDM should request all SLT members be prepared to suggest, at the meeting, specific KPIs that they believe are important enough to be regularly tracked. They should also suggest the frequency of review of the KPIs.

As each suggestion is made, someone will be assigned to write out each of the KPIs on a flip chart for all members to see.

KPI Selection Discussions

When all the suggestions for KPIs are completed, there should be discussions to make the final selections. Your SLT should first discuss the KPIs that need to be tracked and monitored monthly or annually that track critical components, whether Goal or Action Plans, of your Organization Plans. These KPIs are referred to as Plan Specific KPIs.

Only after the discussion and selection of Plan Specific KPIs should there be a discussion of a second set of KPIs—Perennial KPIs—that are not important measurements of any of your Organization Plans but, nevertheless, important to monitor. I will discuss Perennial KPIs later in this chapter.

Each suggested KPI on the flip-chart list needs to be discussed, one by one. During the KPI selection discussions, each SLT member who suggested a KPI should be given time to explain why he or she believes it is important that the SLT monitor the suggested KPI and whether they see the KPI as an important Plan Specific KPI.

Warning: it is not unusual for members to take the conversation away from discussions of selecting KPIs to a discussion about quotas and minimum acceptable results for these KPIs. This meeting is not the time to determine such quotas or minimum acceptable results. The meeting needs to stay focused on identifying the KPIs.

The discussions about each suggested KPI should ascertain such factors as to whether the KPI meets the qualifications to be a Plan Specific KPI versus a KPI that should be monitored only by a particular SLT member (and not the entire SLT). It is common for a SLT member to suggest a KPI that should be reviewed by the suggesting member but is not a KPI that needs to be reviewed by the SLT.

For example, during the SLT Meeting of a financial services company, the number of new clients acquired for the last month versus last year's performance for the same month was identified as a Plan Specific KPI that contained critical measurements for one of its Organization Plans.

Practical Limitations

There should be consideration of practical limitations such as how many Plan Specific KPIs can be monitored at Organization Plan Monitoring Meetings. The rule of thumb used by many is that all the KPIs should be able to be flash reviewed within five to ten minutes. This flash review time is separate to discussions that may take place if the indicators are of concern. Many organization SLTs limit the total number of Plan Specific KPIs looked at during their monthly meetings to no more than 10 to 15.

The discussions should also consider such practical limitations as:

- Are there practical limitations to the amount of organization manpower that can be allocated to put together the information for the KPIs?
- Is there availability of the information needed for specific KPIs? For instance, you may not want a KPI of "popular rating among affluent customers" because this would be very difficult to measure. It is critical that the KPI is 100% accurate. The underlying data has to be completely reliable.
- What should be the frequency of monitoring each of the KPIs by the SLT? Typically KPIs are designated to be monitored by the SLT once a month, once a quarter, or annually. Most KPIs will be reviewed at each Organization Plan Monitoring Meeting. In some cases, the type of information for a KPI may only be available annually, such as information comparing your annual results to competitors' based upon information your competitors may be required to share by law.
- Does your organization have a way to measure the KPI? You wouldn't want to design a KPI for increasing customer satisfaction, for example, unless you had a way to measure and track customer satisfaction; such as with a validated survey system.

Getting Agreement On Plan Specific KPIs

The primary objective of the meeting is to get agreement on which

Plan Specific KPIs should be monitored. Plan Specific KPIs show the progress of specific results of measurable things that are tied to key business processes and operational activities that support an Action Plan or an Organization Goal. Each Plan Specific KPI needs to be presented as a comparison versus projected results so that at every Organization Plan Monitoring Meeting, the SLT can track the progress of the Organization Plan. Monitoring Plan Specific KPIs helps keep the SLT in the loop as to the actual results versus expected results.

If the SLT is not in full agreement on a Plan Specific KPI, it is up to the KDM to make the final decision.

Getting Agreement On Plan Specific KPIs

After identifying the Plan Specific KPIs your SLT should monitor, it is time to select non-Plan-Specific KPIs. I refer to these as Perennials and discuss them later in this chapter. Some, if not most, of the selected KPIs to be reviewed by the SLT will not be Plan Specific KPIs.

KPIs Selected Should Be Expressed In A Way That Is Easily Understood

Your selected KPIs should be expressed in a way that is easily understood by all your employees, not just your SLT. For instance, if your finance company allows you a credit line based on 80 percent of the number of units in inventory, you might want to express this as "The company credit line usage is 94.8% of the allowable limit," as opposed to "The company credit line is at $347,000 on a current inventory value of $458,000" which is difficult to interpret in terms of performance.

KPIs Are Measured Against Something

Usually KPIs are measured against something (e.g. sales against same month last year and against budget). A number by itself is just data. But comparisons and ratios, on the other hand, provide information about how your organization is performing in specific areas compared to expectations.

You may measure your KPI performance against internal expectations or against outside data points such as tracking your KPIs versus industry norms. If your KPI is versus industry norms, ask "What industries does our work come from? What sources measure the ***Industry and Economic Trends*** statistics we need?"

KPIs Don't Have To Be Forever

If you find that a KPI is not giving you actionable information or is no longer relevant, get rid of it. If a KPI is related to a specific plan that is no longer in effect, you may want to stop tracking the KPI or you may want to treat it as a Perennial KPI, which is explained below.

Perennial KPIs

As I mentioned earlier, there is a type of KPI that is not specific/critical to a Goal or Action Plan that is part of an Organization Plan. This KPI, which is referred to as a Perennial KPI, shows the progress of certain essential results of the organization and needs to be monitored for an indefinite period of time.

Perennial KPIs are typically sent to and reviewed by managers or teams of managers that need the KPI information in order to most effectively manage their areas of responsibility. Perennial KPIs may be monitored by those getting the information, by the recipients just reading it and/or by specifically calling meetings, as needed, to review these Perennial KPIs.

Perennial KPIs should be "big picture" in that they provide a high-level snapshot of success for the overall organization or some aspect of the organization. These KPIs track critical processes and results in your organization. Some Perennial KPIs are very common, regardless of the type of business, such as the KPI of the number of new accounts opened in the last month and for the year to date versus last year for same time frames.

On the other hand, there are Perennial KPIs that are important only to specific organizations based upon their particular needs. The examples below might be very important to some institutions but meaningless to others.

- The number of weeks of backlog of order against the optimum range of weeks.
- Revenue generated per field technician versus industry average.

It's important that your organization identify which Perennial KPIs are necessary. Not identifying the right Perennial KPIs can cause problems. For example, a particular financial ratio may be important to your organization but not important to others.

The SLT of one organization did not monitor the ratio of the company's current assets versus current liabilities. It so happens that the company's loan documents required a minimum current ratio. The current ratio, as show on the company's annual financial statement, was in violation of the lending requirement. When the lender saw the current ratio was below their requirements, it caused all sorts of problems for the company. This problem would not have happened if the current ratio KPI had been identified as a KPI to be monitored throughout the year by the SLT. Steps could have easily been taken that would have brought the current ratio into compliance for the bank loan.

CHAPTER 14

Most Common KPIs Selected

The following are among the most common KPIs tracked by SLTs:

- A KPI that indicates customer or client prospects in the organization pipeline last month versus for the same month last year. This KPI is an indicator of the *Pipeline* for new work in the immediate or near future. It is typical to also have some KPI relating to movement of these prospects into a later stage of becoming a client.
- A KPI that indicates operating efficiency such as production per labor hour, profit per unit of production, gross margin ROI, inventory turns, labor to expense ratios and breakeven multiples.
- A KPI that indicates how well we do what we do from a quality standpoint, such as complaint ratios, errors per units delivered, jobs over budget or return ratios.

Common Sales Related KPIs

The following sales-related KPIs are some of the more common KPIs tracked:

- Number of Leads
- Number of Calls
- Number of Contacts
- Contact Rate
- Number of First Appointments
- Sign-up rate
- Appointments Kept
- % of Appointments Kept
- Appointments Cancelled/No Show
- % of Appointments Cancelled
- Second Appointments Scheduled
- Second Appointment Rate
- Second Appointment Kept
- Second Appointment Kept Rate
- Clients Signed

Expense-to-Sales Ratios KPIs

There are various KPI ratios that compare specific expense items to net sales. One such KPI is the percentage of depreciation, depletion, and amortization to sales ratio, which is the annual depreciation, amortization and depletion expenses divided by net sales, then multiplied by 100.

Other Commonly Tracked KPIs

- Gross revenue
- Net revenue
- Cost of sales
- Customer evaluations of service or products
- % of products returned

Financial Ratios KPIs

Many lenders and companies that extend credit require minimum ratios, and your organization needs to monitor these ratios. One of the most common ratios for such required minimums is the Current Ratio, which is the total current assets divided by total current liabilities. For example:

- $200,000 total current assets / $200,000 total current liabilities = 1 to 1 ratio

The current ratio gives an indication of a firm's ability to service its current obligations. The higher the current ratio, the greater the "cushion" between current obligations and a firm's ability to pay them. Of course, the composition and quality of current assets is also a critical factor in the analysis of a firm's liquidity.

Another major liquidity ratio is the quick ratio, also referred to as the "acid test". The quick ratio is the cash and equivalents plus accounts and notes receivable (trade) divided by total current liabilities.

- Cash & equivalents + accounts & notes (trade) / Total current liabilities

The quick ratio shows how well an organization's current liabilities are covered by its most liquid current assets. A quick ratio of less than 1-1 indicates a "dependency" on inventory or other current assets to liquidate short-term debt.

Another of the most common ratios important to many lenders is your inventory-turn ratio. Your inventory-turn ratio is the cost of sales divided by inventory.

- Cost of Sales / Inventory

This ratio measures the number of times your inventory turns over during a year. A low inventory turnover by industry standards may indicate poor liquidity, possible over-stocking or obsolescence of your inventory. One problem with this ratio is that it compares one day's inventory to cost of goods sold and does not take seasonal fluctuations into account.

Key Point: Your inventory turn might be dramatically different if the end of a different month is used; i.e., December 31 instead of March 31. Consider using a year-end that will offer the best inventory turn ratio. One organization turned a three-times ratio to a four-times ratio by changing its year-end by two months.

Coverage Ratios

Another set of ratios looked at by lenders is referred to as the coverage ratios. They measure your firm's ability to service its interest payments. An example is the ratio of earnings before interest and taxes (EBIT). Interest ratio is the earnings (profit) before annual interest expense and taxes divided by the annual interest expense.

Earnings Before Interest & Taxes / Annual Interest Expense

Leverage Ratios

Highly leveraged firms, those with heavy debt in relation to their net worth, are viewed as more vulnerable to negative changes, such as greater competition or business downturns, than those with lower debt to worth positions. There are two leverage ratios that most lenders and those extending credit will look at to see how your organization compares to your industry. These are the fixed-assets-to-worth ratio and the debt-to-worth ratio.

The fixed assets-to-worth ratio is the fixed assets (net of accumulated depreciation) divided by tangible net worth.

- Net Fixed Assets / Tangible Net Worth

This ratio measures the extent to which an owner's equity (capital) has been invested in plant and equipment (fixed assets). A lower ratio indicates a proportionately smaller investment in fixed assets in relation to net worth, and a better "cushion" for creditors in case of liquidation.

NOTE: If your fixed-assets-to-worth ratio compares poorly with your industry, review how heavily you rely on leasing compared to others in your industry. The presence of substantial leased fixed assets (as shown on the balance sheet) by others in your industry may deceptively lower this ratio.

The debt-to-worth-ratio is the total liabilities of your organization divided by its tangible net worth.

- Total Liabilities / Tangible Net Worth

This ratio expresses the relationship between capital contributed by creditors and that contributed by owners. A firm with a low debt/worth ratio compared to its industry is interpreted as having greater ability to borrow.

Operating Ratios

There is another group of ratios, referred to generally as Operating Ratios, which are used to evaluate how your operating performance compares to others in your industry. The most commonly used operating ratios are: percentage-of-profits-before-taxes-to-tangible-net-worth ratio, and the sales-to-total-assets ratio.

The-percentage-of-profits-before-taxes-to-tangible-net-worth ratio is your profit before taxes divided by tangible net worth, then multiplied by 100.

- Profit Before Taxes / Tangible Net Worth x 100

Many analysts believe this ratio measures the productive use of your firm's fixed assets.

Key Point: Largely depreciated fixed assets cause a distortion of this ratio. Point this out to potential lenders and investors if your ratio is poor by industry standards.

The-sales-to-total-assets ratio is your net sales divided by your total assets.

Net Sales / Total Assets

It is used to compare organizations within specific industry groups as to their effective employment of assets.

CHAPTER 15

Examples of Actual KPIs Monitored by Different Organizations

Example Of Selected Training Organization KPIs

The following is an example of KPIs selected for tracking sales-related Tactics of an Action Plan with an objective of increasing annual sales revenue to US$2,000,000 within two years:

- Average sale/number of sales per week actual versus projected of 2.5
- Sales Close rate with prospects met actual versus projected of 50%
- Appointments set per day actual versus projected of 1
- Cold calls made to set per appointment actual versus projected of 50

Example of Technology Service Company KPI

A technology service company records all discussions with customers about equipment and service upgrades in their CRM system and considers them prospects in the pipeline. Those prospects who request written proposals from the company are weighted as a percentage of total prospects that came into the pipeline.

Example Accounting Firm KPIs

Month vs. Month comparison of:

- Number of active clients
- Average retention period of clients
- New clients signed
- Client re-signs
- Average billing per client
- Total Fees Collected

Example of Financial Services Company

Each of the KPIs below relate to measurements in Action Plans found in one of the two Organization Plans for a financial services company. One Organization Plan is Client related and the other involves expansion of territories in which they operate:

KPIs for Financial Company's Client Related Organization Plan

1. Last month's client information versus same month last year, by country:

   - Total number of paying clients
   - Average revenue per client
   - Average months of client retention
   - Average active clients per unit for units operating more than 12 months from completing Initial Training

2. Total number of new clients acquired company wide for running

12-month period ending last month versus previous year, separately classified by:

- Referrals
- Networking
- Other tactics

3. New territory launch metrics per territory for running 12-month period ending last month versus previous year, separately classified by:

- Contact rate of talking to prospects
- Scheduled Discovery Meeting appointments
- Kept Appointments
- Requests for second meeting appointments (RFAs)
- Kept RFA meetings
- New client applications signed

4. Average number of clients for new territories for current calendar year versus previous calendar year, separately classified based on membership at:

- Sixth full month from completion of Initial Training
- Twelfth full month from completion of Initial Training

KPIs For Financial Company's Territories-Related Organization plan

1. Number of new-signed unit territories by country for calendar year, month to date versus previous year through same month, separately classified by:

- Unit Franchisees
- Company owned

2. Number of lost unit territories by country for calendar year, month to date versus previous year through same month, separately classified by:

- Unit Franchisees
- Company owned

3. Number of new-signed unit territories by country for calendar year required by development schedule, versus previous calendar year through same month, separately classified by:

- Unit Franchisees
- Company owned

4. Total number of new territory prospects as of end of last month, versus same month previous year, by country, separately classified by:

- Franchise prospects in pipeline
- Company territory prospects in pipeline
- Franchise prospects with confirmed scheduled Discovery Days
- Company territory prospects with confirmed scheduled Discovery Days

CHAPTER 16

KPI Presentation Format

Ideally, all monthly KPIs will be shown in the form of a dashboard "flash" report, giving SLT members a quick understanding of how the KPIs are progressing or can be expected to perform in the near future.

As technology becomes more capable of measuring results, it is easy and inexpensive to use computer-generated measurement dashboards comparing projected KPI results versus actual KPI measurement results. There are web-based applications, for example, that have "landing pages" with a dashboard that will indicate the progress on each of the Action Plans for your Organization Plans.

If you want to know the status of each Tactic for each of your Action Plans, Dashboards can provide a summary of the state of each Tactic of each of your Actions. These applications can make it easy to flash view progress by showing a red highlight if an action has not been started, yellow when an item is partially completed, and green when the item is fully completed for each Action Plan.

After you have identified the KPIs your SLT wants to track, consider how you would group them for display and monitoring. One company that uses a dashboard to track Sales KPIs, shows KPIs grouped by five related factors: (1) Mailers (2) Telemarketing (3) Seminar Presentations (4) Referrals and (5) Emails. The SLT regularly reviews the Dashboard, which they refer to as their company Wheel of Fortune, for the KPI for each of the five sales factors, to determine the company sales trend.

If you don't want to use web-based applications to track Organization Plans, including the tracking of all of the Action Plans, it is easy to create the statements via Excel spreadsheets or even Word documents that can provide simple, clear and concise KPI information.

Spending a very small amount of time to put in place a Dashboard for KPIs you have identified, using easily accessible technology, or customized Excel spreadsheets or word documents with customized groupings, will save your SLT many hours because of the quick flash-type review that Dashboards make possible.

Now It's Time To Get Results

Now that you know how to create your Organization Plans and iden-tify KPIs, let's look at what it takes to get results execution.

SECTION 6

Execution Role of SLT

Many organizations have spent a lot of SLT time discussing what needs to be done and coming up with great Organization Plans that are based on an endless supply of "great ideas," but never bring about the desired results because they don't commit the time and dedication needed to execute the Organization Plans. Without great execution, great Organization Plans will not bring about great results. A SLT that does not value Execution Commitment to Strategies and Action Plans is preparing for its organization's decline.

For strategic planning to be effective, all members of your SLT must be committed to execution (Execution Commitment). Execution Commitment directly connects the act of *setting goals to achieving goals*. Each SLT member must clearly understand his or her strategic planning role, which includes being fully committed to the strategic planning process and making the Plans succeed.

One of the marks of high-impact organizations is that they produce tangible results from their Organization Plans with strong Execution Commitment. This section will cover the required involvement, methods to use and expectations of the SLT for bringing about these results.

CHAPTER 17

Monthly SLT Meetings

Projected results don't always happen the way you would want. That's just a fact of life for any organization, whether small or large. When you hold Organization Plan Monitoring Meetings to focus on the implementation of your Organization Plans, there is a greater likelihood your organization will be reacting to situations faster, with more flexibility and more aggressiveness than if you do not have a scheduled time to meet to focus on their progress.

The focus of your Organization Plan Monitoring Meetings is to achieve the Goal of each of your Organization Plans. There are two steps for the meetings with this focus in mind. The first is that your SLT members unemotionally evaluate whether their Organization Plans are working. The second objective is to discuss possible adjustments and changes, if needed, that can be done in a timely manner.

If your Organization Plan Monitoring Meetings are on schedule, structured right and facilitated well, the time spent at these meetings will be among the most important things your SLT does to bring about successful execution of your Organization Plans.

Meeting Logistics

Your Organization Plan Monitoring Meetings should be scheduled to take place at the same time each month, such as the last Wednesday of every month. Organization Plan Monitoring Meetings are usually held at the organization's offices, but with all employees understanding the meetings are to be without interruptions.

The meetings should be scheduled for the same amount of time each month, such as four hours or eight hours of meeting time. I view four hours as the minimum necessary to ensure the meeting is effective and recommend a full day if possible.

Evaluate Results Of Organization Plans

During Organization Plan Monitoring Meetings, your SLT will monitor whether your Organization Plans are working properly, including the validity of Strategies and the Action Plans that ultimately lead to the achievement of Goals.

The progress of each Action Plan should be considered by the SLT both from a standpoint of the associated KPI and also the information from a verbal, and sometimes also written, report by the Responsible Party for the Action Plan. If unexpected roadblocks have emerged, the Responsible Party, who is accountable for the project, needs to inform the other SLT members of this situation at the Organization Plan Monitoring Meetings.

The KPIs that your SLT are monitoring and reports by the Responsible Parties for Action Plans should be considered by the SLT at each monthly meeting. The Responsible Party for the completion of an Action Plan needs to provide updates on how things are progressing in relation to the time goals of the Action Plan. Key Action Plan benchmarks met or missed should be proactively reported, rather than glossed over, so the SLT knows if things are going as planned or not.

The reporting by the Responsible Party should include visual handouts with graphs or charts, if possible. One organization requires Responsible Parties for Action Plans to color code the actual versus predicted results with yellow if they were close and green if the results met or exceeded the forecast, or red if the Action Plan committed results were missed. When results are shown in red, the KDM asks the Responsible Party to explain why predicted results for those actions were not achieved, and there is usually a SLT discussion of the situation.

It may seem obvious, but make sure you are getting actual results from the Responsible Party that are based upon the same factors the SLT had in mind when it determined the projected results. Sometimes information reported may be misleading, although there may have been no intention to mislead.

For example, the Sales Manager of an organization was the Responsible Party for an Action Plan that involved signing new clients. The results shared at an Organization Plan Monitoring Meeting looked even better than the projected results of the Action Plan. The CEO commented at the team meeting when he heard the number of new clients, "Wow, we are really doing well." These type of great results were reported for a few months until a question was asked that resulted in the SLT finding that the reported information was based on signed client agreements without payments ever being generated from the new clients.

The timing of the SLT knowing about roadblocks to progress of an Action Plan is important. If roadblock information is shared early enough, Action Plans can often be changed so the roadblocks don't impact the timely and successful completion of the project. If not shared early enough, it could result in not being able to make changes in time to achieve Action Plan success.

One Responsible Party for an Action Plan had a deadline of June 1 to complete a customized fabrication piece for a design project with benchmark results to take place by March, April and May. At the March and April Monthly SLT Meetings, this Responsible Party reported to the SLT that his Action Plan was right on target. Unfortunately, the SLT never required KPIs from the Responsible Party to demonstrate the specific progress on the Plan.

Weeks before the entire project was to be completed, the Responsible Party for an Action Plan fired an employee who was working on the

Action Plan. The fired employee contacted the KDM to let her know that there was no way the project was going to be completed by the due date. When the KDM asked the Responsible Party, she responded that it was true the commitment date would not be made but that she was going to let the team know about it at the June meeting. Unfortunately, the Action Plan failed because required results didn't occur within the specified timeframe.

When your SLT is doing its monthly progress reviews of Action Plans, it will commonly ask questions of the Responsible Party. The questions will primarily focus on progress toward the objectives of each Action Plan or lack thereof, rather than on detailed updates on the progress of each of the Tactics for the Action Plan. Getting down to the level of Tactics is more of an unusual occurrence rather than a monthly-meeting pattern.

Your SLT meetings are to be high level and strategic. Spending time reviewing Tactics will stop the SLT from fulfilling their responsibilities on a strategic level. Significant SLT involvement by requesting the Responsible Party update them on all the Tactics of each Action Plan would not be a good use of the team members' time.

If your SLT meetings allocate time to monitor/review how every task is doing with every Tactic, not much would get done in the meeting at a strategic level. There would just not be sufficient meeting time available to focus on the things on which the SLT should be focusing. Consider that one of your Goals has five Strategies, and each of the Strategies has five Action Plans, then the 25 Action Plans together might have hundreds of Tactics in total.

> *Don't let SLT meetings get tied up in minutia. These meetings are not intended to track the status of each listed Tactic in each Action Plan.*

However, there may be times when a deep review of Tactics for a specific Action Plan is requested because of problems with the progress of the Action Plan, and the potential changes necessary are "deep" within the Tactics of the Action Plans.

Eliminate, Change Or Add Strategies

Your SLT should be monitoring monthly whether Strategies are moving towards achieving the Goal for which the Strategies were developed. If the answer is no, it is time for the SLT to rethink the Strategies. Things change, and changed circumstances often require a modification of a current Strategy or the implementation of a different Strategy for achieving your Goal.

What may have seemed like a great Strategy may no longer be the right Strategy. It does not matter whether Strategies seemed like the best Strategies for your organization at the time they were created. When you recognize they are no longer the right Strategies, it is the responsibility of the SLT to do something about it. One strategic change alone can have a major impact upon the success of a Goal.

Usually, when a Strategy is not succeeding, it is because the Action Plans for it are not working. However, there may be situations where Action Plans for a Strategy are succeeding, but the Strategy is not. In this case, the problem is not the Action Plans but the Strategy they are meant to fulfill. The Strategy may need to be modified, eliminated or replaced. When a Strategy is modified, eliminated or replaced, you will typically need to develop revised or new Action Plans.

Sometimes the problem is that the organization is working on more Strategies than it can handle. One organization had five Strategies for one Goal with five Action Plans for each Strategy. The twenty-five Action Plans totally overwhelmed two of the Responsible Parties for Actions Plans to a point where very little was accomplished, and the Responsible Parties were de-motivated. The due dates on the Action Plans of these two parties were constantly missed.

The Two Responsible Parties discussed this problem at an Organization Plan Monitoring Meeting. They both expressed their view to the other SLT members that there was no way all of the Action Plans for which they were responsible were going to be accomplished. This led to a discussion that resulted in the SLT eliminating all but two of the Strategies. Eliminating these two Strategies resulted in eliminating 10 Action Plans. This change allowed the two

Responsible Parties to focus and achieve the desired results for the remaining Strategies.

Another example of a strategy being revised, along with related Action Plans, involved an organization that had not achieved its Goal of a specific increase in sales for the year. In fact, it had actually experienced decreased sales compared to the previous year.

When discussing the lack of success of Strategies for the Plan, one of the SLT members pointed out that "what had happened in the last year that was different" was that the KDM had stopped allocating a portion of her time to her signing up new major accounts. The KDM explained to her team that she had intentionally cut back on the time she spent meeting with new account prospects in order to spend more time on other company-related activities that she considered more CEO in nature.

The problem was that her selling ability and ability to get in front of potential large accounts was responsible for opening many new major accounts in the past. None of the sales employees, many of whom had been with the company for years, had demonstrated the ability to close major accounts the way she had done.

Her SLT recommended they create a new Strategy to recruit a heavy-weight salesperson, with the KDM reallocating more time for personal sales effort until the new employee demonstrated a certain level of results. Another new Strategy was to get her back to spending significant time meeting major account prospects, with a company salesperson making calls to set up the appointments for her.

The Action Plan deadline was twelve months from the creation of the Action Plan, which she thought would be enough time to get company sales back on track. Another member of the SLT was responsible for an Action Plan to hire and train the new salesperson. Within months of the KDM reallocating her work time, the company's sales were back on track with the sales-plan projections. At the same time, the hiring of new salespeople took place pursuant to an Action Plan that also called for better sales training and sales tools for the new employees and all their salespeople.

Eliminate, Change Or Add an Action Plan For a Current Strategy

After your SLT members review the Plan KPIs being monitored for an Action Plan and hear the report from the Responsible Party on a specific Action Plan, it is time for SLT discussions about Action Plan progress. If there appears to be lack of adequate progress for an Action Plan, it should trigger SLT discussions about required changes. The team may decide to modify, eliminate or add Action Plans to the particular Strategy.

Although there will be times that SLT members provide suggestions for specific Tactics, the SLT typically will not spend much monthly meeting time on suggestions for specific Tactics. The SLT will usually keep their suggestions at a higher level than suggestions about such things as who should do a specific task for a Tactic to be implemented.

Monthly Management Team Meeting Charter

Some organizations hand out a monthly management team charter at the beginning of each of the Organization Plan Monitoring Meetings to remind SLT members what is expected of them at these meetings. The following is an example of such a charter.

"To facilitate success, you, as a management team attendee at our monthly management team meetings, will exercise self-discipline, perseverance and an ability to focus your energies to satisfying what is most important for our company. No matter how important your day-to-day company responsibilities, you will keep focus during the monthly meetings on achieving the Goals expressed in the Organization Plans developed by the management team."

CHAPTER 18

Plan Resources Allocation

Successful execution of an Organization Plan requires organization resources to be allocated to the plan. When the SLT first creates an Organization Plan, it usually has only a "ballpark" idea about what resources may be needed to implement the plan.

When developing the budget for an Organization Plan, it is important to consider all human and financial resources realistically needed for each Action Plan to succeed. Consequently, the first budget is not typically done until all Action Plans for all Strategies in the Organization Plan are fully developed. Only after the proposed Action Plans are completed, with all necessary Tactics, can you forecast and budget your foreseeable financial requirements for the particular plan with some degree of clarity. In addition to the financial factors, you will, at that point, know how to estimate the amount of the Responsible Party's time and his or her department's time as it will need to be diverted to work on the Organization Plan.

This budget of financial and human resources may need to be revised once implementation gets under way. At that time, you will know what Action Plans, or even Tactics within them, are working and what is not working.

At all times there should be one or two Organization Plan(s) on which your SLT is focused. These are the plans that address your organization's DCSF(s). This plan or plans need to receive your organization's greatest allocation of resources: including human resources, equipment capacity and financial resources.

Because there will be uncertainty regarding resource allocation until implementation of Action Plans has started, it is usually best not to implement any Organization Plans beyond the plans that address your organization's DCSF(s). Once these plans are running, you will have a clearer idea of what resources remain and what are needed for the less important Organization Plans.

Too Many Organization Plans

It's not uncommon for an organization's SLT to decide that two different goals are both equally important and are thus the driving Goals. In such cases, the SLT creates and implements two Organization Plans. However, I believe that two Organization Plans is the most any organization should start implementing.

Some organizations have thought that their organization had the resources to successfully start with as many as five Organization Plans and put them all in play at once. In each case that I am aware of, it turned out that the organizations did not have resources, usually the human resources, for all of them to be implemented. The result was failure for all of the Organization Plans.

Better to Succeed With One or Two Organization Plans Than Fail With Several

In one case, the organization's controller expressed the opinion at an Organization Plan Monitoring Meeting that the company was spreading company resources, human and financial, across too many different Action Plans. The SLT decided there would be a postponing of all but two of the Organization Plans. Results for the remaining plans picked up almost immediately.

Smaller Organizations

The approach of first trying to implement one, or at most two, of your most important Organization Plans before implementing another Organization Plan is particularly important for smaller organizations. This is because they are less likely to have a large number of managers who are able to allocate time to working on Organization Plans. In addition, the smaller the organization, the more likely it is the organization will have less financial resources available for implementing multiple plans.

CHAPTER 19

Getting Plans Embraced by the Entire Organization

Regardless of the type or size of your organization, you and the other members of your Strategic Leadership Team are the catalyst for change in your organization. However, alignment of the SLT in support of Organization Plans is not enough. The SLT must ingrain the importance of strategic planning execution into your organization's culture, and it is especially important to get support from all employees for the Goal for the driving Organization Plan(s).

All members of your SLT need to be promoting awareness and both showing and getting support for all your employees for the Organization Plan(s). This requires awareness of the Goal and, in most cases, the Strategies for achieving the Goal. This awareness must reach everyone in your organization so that your whole organization is on the same page.

Your SLT is responsible for getting the support throughout your organization for your Organization Plans. Without the Organization Plan(s) being embraced at all levels of your organization, including

> *Your Organization Plans need to be embraced throughout your organization to provide your organization with a solid foundation for achieving its greatest level of success.*

the lowest levels, great strategic planning results are not likely to happen. This organization-wide support will not happen unless all your SLT members communicate to non-SLT employees in a way that shows they support your Organization Plans. This is essential, whether or not the SLT member originally supported the plans when the SLT was discussing and developing them.

Creating Organization Plan Awareness

Once the SLT has developed an Organization Plan and the Action Plans have also been identified, it's important to communicate them consistently and continually to employees who may have any level of impact on the results.

Your SLT's communication objective is to bring about a high level of organization-wide awareness, commitment and focus on the Goal or Goals of your driving Organization Plan(s).

The Goal(s) should be so well known that they become like a well-memorized mantra for all your employees. You should be able to ask any employee to tell you the organization's driving Goal or Goals and get at least a good paraphrased answer.

Also consider communicating possible financial rewards to your employees if a Goal or significant benchmarks for the Goal are met.

Financial Reward To Employees That Connect To Results For Plans

No matter how important the Goal to your organization, some employees will think, "That's great — achieving the Goal is going to be more work for me, and when it does work, there will be more profits, and the executives will get bigger bonuses, but what's in it for me." You have the power to overcome this thinking by creating employee rewards that can be earned when the Goal is achieved or when benchmarks toward the Goal are achieved. Consider incentives that are tied to achieving the Goal results.

For a for-profit company, greater profits from achieving a Goal should result in greater sharing, with possible financial incentives for the organization's employees, whether management or non-management. This should be done with measurable performance reviews that use objective KPIs. The financial rewards to the employees do not have to be large for them to be effective in gaining employee support.

One manufacturing organization identified department-related benchmarks for every department responsible for any of the Action Plans created to achieve the Goal of its driving Plan. For each quarter that an individual department reached its Action Plan benchmark, $50.00 per employee was given to each non-management employee in the department. This incentive proved to be motivating to the non-management employees.

The KDM of a retail chain announced to his store employees that they would each receive a dinner for two, at any one of six particular restaurants, if the retail chain achieved a specific organization Goal by a stated deadline. This organization received great storewide "buy in" with this relatively inexpensive storewide reward program. The retail chain also successfully used tickets to baseball games when quarterly benchmarks were met along the way toward achieving the Goal.

Develop A Strategy To Get Employee Support For A Goal

The following are some of the communication methods and tools your SLT can use to get employee support for a Goal.

Signs And Graphs Placed On Your Organization Walls

Display a sign of the Goal on various walls around the organization in places employees are likely to see, such as hallways, break rooms, lunchrooms. Also display a chart that shows Goal progress, and keep the information up-to-date with periodic updates.

One manufacturing company displayed the Goal of its driving

Organization SLT Plan on posters in the company lunchroom. The posters stated: "Increase Company gross profits by 3 percent by April 20XX." Next to each poster, a graph was put up that showed the results needed every three months in order to be on track to achieve the Goal and also the actual results for the three months that were just completed.

Communicating the Goal In Writing To Non-SLT Employees

One of the SLT members should draft or be responsible for assigning someone to draft a written communication to send to your employees. One of your main objectives in the communication should be showing employees how achieving the Goal supports and benefits the organization. If the benefit will be for every department and every employee at every level, this should be stated.

When every employee knows the Goal of your driving Organization Plan(s), it is much more likely that those involved in the Action Plans will take ownership of those areas they or their departments are responsible for.

Before sending the written communication, get feedback on the draft of communications from your entire SLT. If done right, this type of communication helps bring about a greater buy in from your employees, and they are more likely to do what it takes for the Plan to succeed.

The delivery method for this written communication about the driving Goal(s) may be through paper handout or email. This communication needs to be reinforced with an in-person group meeting, which I will discuss later.

Employee Group Meetings

One way to get employee buy in is to hold scheduled employee group meetings to discuss the driving Goal on which you want company-wide support. If your KDM is a decent public speaker, it is best that he or she give the group presentation. Also, all SLT members should be present at the meetings. Having the SLT members at the group meetings will help show their full support.

This type of employee group meeting will ensure employees know the desired company direction and will encourage their alignment with it. It will also show you value the views of your employees.

During these group meetings, allocate time for your employees to ask questions, make suggestions and express their views about the Goal and about any strategies or Action Plans you share with them.

> *The group meeting to discuss your driving company Goal will reduce any stress your employees feel about the "unknowns" they have about the direction of the company.*

One company had a group meeting with all of its 50 mid-level and frontline employees to inform them about the organization's Goal and the strategies for the Goal. The KDM conducted the meeting, and all SLT members were present.

The KDM's presentation was motivational, using Power Point slides and videos to bring about employee excitement for the Goal. After the presentation, she explained she wanted to tap into their ideas for ways that could improve the chances of success of the Strategies for the Goal. She said those who didn't feel comfortable sharing their views during the meeting could send their suggestions directly to her. She also promised financial rewards for suggestions submitted that were used.

The KDM requested the suggestions go directly to her out of concern that immediate managers may not see the value in the suggestions that she and the other SLT members would consider valuable. The immediate managers might therefore not pass these suggestions on to the SLT.

Questions For Determining Your Best Employee Communications Strategy For A Goal

Answering the following questions will help your organization determine the best way to communicate your driving Goal throughout all employee levels of your organization:

1. Who should do the communicating? It may be you, or you may decide to delegate this responsibility.

2. What level of details of the Organization Driving Goal do you want to share?

3. What methods and tools of communication will be most effective to clearly express the organization Driving Goal information to all relevant parties?

4. At what physical location(s) should the communication take place—does your organization have several locations or more than one meeting area in your location?

5. With what size groups should you meet? Effective communication may not be possible with too big a group. Meeting with smaller groups using different communication methods may prove more effective.

6. Do you want to open the meetings to discussions by employees relating to the Driving Goal, and if so, what format should you use for facilitating the group discussions?

7. Should the communications be virtual or tangible?

Communicating Aligned Support By Co-KDMs

Some organizations have Co-KDMs such as Co-CEOs or co-owners with equal ownership. If the organization has Co-KDMs and one of them comes across as less than fully supportive of an Organization Plan, it poses special challenges. Once the SLT commits to an Organization Plan, the Co-KDMs must get in alignment and communicate support with a common voice. They must each be totally committed to execution of the Organization Plan.

Co-KDMs also need to show full support for the execution of the plans with their actions, not just with words. Once Organization Plans are finalized, a Co- KDM who did not like a plan when the plan was in the discussions stage at the SLT meetings should not share with any employees the dissent that the Co-KDM may have had.

This showing of Co-KDM alignment is essential so that all employees "row in the same direction". If any SLT members or other employee senses division between the co-owners and lack of support for a plan, they may not give their full efforts to the plan's success.

SECTION 7

Execution Role of Responsible Parties

You now understand the execution roles of the SLT, as a group. Now let's look at the execution role of Responsible Parties for the Action Plans for which they are responsible. A Responsible Party can be an SLT member but is often a member of their team such as a Marketing Specialist or Customer Service Supervisor. The success of the Action Plans is vital to the success of your Organization Plan(s).

A Responsible Party's role includes communicating with the SLT about the Action Plan(s) they are responsible for. A Responsible Party also must create and manage the Tactics of the Action Plan(s) to which they have committed.

CHAPTER 20

Responsible Party's Interaction with SLT Relating to Action Plan

When a Responsible Party commits to being the Responsible Party for a specific Action Plan, the Responsible Party must do his or her best to make sure the committed Action Plan results happen within the committed time. In addition, the Responsible Party's role includes updating the SLT of the status of any Action Plan(s).

A Responsible Party needs to let your SLT know, in a timely manner, when they need help. Sometimes a Responsible Party may feel the following concerning the Action Plans for which they are responsible:

- Things don't seem to be going as planned–sometimes as the Tactics implementation is taking place.
- The Action Plan is overwhelming.
- They have run out of ideas for getting the committed results.

All of these things need to be communicated to the SLT as soon as possible after a Responsible Party has come to these conclusions. This is usually done by memo prior to an Organization Plan Monitoring

Meeting with a request to schedule time on the agenda that will be devoted to brainstorming ideas and getting suggestions for changes to get results in line with objectives for the Action Plan.

For example, the Marketing Director of a retail chain was the Responsible Party for an Action Plan that involved increasing walk-in traffic-count results to a specific average count for new store openings. After trying different tactics she had developed for the plan, she told the SLT at an Organization Plan Monitoring Meeting that the things she had been trying for the Action Plan were just not working. She admitted she was out of ideas for getting the objective results of the Action Plan and asked for any fresh ideas.

> *Don't avoid asking for help with your Action Plan because you feel bad about asking for help. Asking for and getting help, when appropriate, is okay.*

One of the other SLT members shared a marketing idea from an article he had just read. After discussions, the SLT recommended the Responsible Party try the idea. This idea, which was implemented, turned out to be the lynchpin to the Action Plan succeeding. The interesting thing about the suggestion is that it came from the head of IT, whose background was not in any way related to marketing.

It is a potentially dangerous situation if a person who faces a challenge in meeting a deadline doesn't request help of the SLT until it's too late (or doesn't ask at all). Usually, no SLT will be judgmental or upset when a Responsible Party trying to make a deadline asks for help, provided the person does not have a pattern of missing deadlines. But *every SLT* is likely to be upset if the person who has committed to a deadline repeatedly misses deadlines without asking for help.

Sometimes An Action Plan Needs To Be Put On Pause

There are times a Responsible Party may need to put an Action Plan, or at least key Tactics for the Action Plan, on hold. But this should not be done unless there is full alignment of the SLT.

A Canadian organization purchased materials for parts made by it from a supplier located in China. One day, the Canadian company was informed that operations of the company in China was devastated by an earthquake and delivery of the materials would not resume for a minimum of six months.

The SLT had a meeting, and all agreed that a particular VP of the Canadian organization had to drop all her activities as Responsible Party for certain Action Plans and, instead, focus on finding another supplier who could provide the parts the Chinese company had been supplying. If fabricated material from the new supplier was not available within 90 days, the Canadian organization would have to shut down its parts manufacturing division.

Getting an interim supplier was not easy, because all of the first group of prospective suppliers were unwilling to gear up supply and manufacture the materials needed without receiving a long-term commitment from the Canadian organization. The Canadian organization did not want to give the commitment at first, but ultimately had to do so to get the necessary supplies.

Budget For Action Plan

The Responsible Party for an Action Plan is responsible for giving the SLT an idea of the budget needed to make the Action Plan succeed. The Responsible Party doesn't have to create the financial information him or herself. It's common for a Responsible Party to request help of someone in the organization's finance or accounting department to determine the amount of money to budget for the Action plan.

Sometimes, after implementation of an Action Plan has started, a Responsible Party will realize the human or financial resources budget is not sufficient to allow an Action Plan to succeed. When this is known, the Responsible Party should report this to the SLT at the monthly meeting. The SLT will then decide what to do.

CHAPTER 21

Creating and Managing
Action Plan Tactics

A Responsible Party for an Action Plan is responsible for creating and implementing the Tactics needed for the Action Plan to succeed by the committed date. A Responsible Party will either personally perform the Tactics for the Action Plan or delegate responsibilities.

Delegation of activities for Tactics to those in departments/teams or individual employees who report directly to the Responsible Party, is easy. It is more challenging when employees not reporting to the Responsible Party are required to undertake Action Plan Tactics. This requires cooperation of the managers to whom these other parties report. The KDM may need to get involved if SLT members are not able to resolve situations relating to delegation of an Action Plan Tactic to an employee who does not report to the Responsible Party.

When a Tactic is to be done by someone other than the Responsible Party, it should always be documented as to who the responsible party is and the expectation of their results. This communication, which can be done in an email, should also state the expectations for the results.

Action Plan Update Meetings With Employees Working On Action Plan Tactics

The Responsible Party, of course, knows how he or she is progressing with the Tactics on which he or she is personally working. But all too often, things break down because of lack of disciplined monitoring of the Tactics that are not being done personally by the Responsible Party. Implementation does not always get the planned results.

Responsible Parties should never assume things are going according to plan just because no one is volunteering to say that the expected Tactics results are not happening. The party responsible for a specific Action Plan needs to get regular updates of how Tactics are progressing. This constant monitoring of results by Responsible Parties is essential to make any timely adjustments to Action Plans.

This monitoring of progress should take place at regularly scheduled meetings (Action Plan Update Meetings) attended by a Responsible Party and the employees or groups of employees involved in carrying out the specific Tactics for the Action Plan. Ideally these meetings will take place weekly until the Action Plan is accomplished. These meetings can be group and/or one-on-one meetings.

These regularly scheduled meetings help keep employees focused on accomplishing the Tactics on which they are working. They will also provide the Responsible Party with an update on the status of actual results versus projected results for each of the delegated Tactics. If creation of materials is involved in the Tactics, the party implementing the Tactics should be asked to demonstrate the progress made on the Tactics, rather than just report the status.

Advantage Of Group Action Plan Update Meetings

One of the advantages of group Action Plan Update Meetings is that great advice may come from an employee not as knowledgeable in a particular area as the person finding challenges completing a particular Tactic. The best and most creative ideas for solving the Tactic problems may come from someone whose organization roles do not involve the areas of the Tactic's challenges.

Advantage Of One-On-One Action Plan Update Meetings

Action Plan Update Meetings do not have to be limited to group meetings with all those working on the Action Plan. With some employees, it's more likely you will get them to become more open in one-on-one Action Plan Update Meetings. Some subordinate employees may be reluctant to voice their opinions, suggestions and constructive criticism in a group setting.

When forecast results have not been achieved, the Responsible Party may also find it easier to get the person implementing the Tactics to explain why predicted results were not achieved and what should be done about it in a one-on-one.

Finding Out Why Results Are Not Tracking

If it comes out at a meeting that results for certain Tactics are not tracking as expected, the Responsible Party should ask why they think certain specific results aren't tracking as projected. Tactics are much more likely to succeed if you get ideas and other feedback from your employees relating to the Tactics assigned to them. These meetings often result in information of which the Responsible Party for the Action Plan was not aware. This information often leads to modifications, revisions and adjusting of Tactics in order to make them more effective.

The need for changes is sometimes uncovered after implementing Tactics that would not have been known before implementation started. In some cases, the Tactics do not need to be changed but timeline commitments may need to be changed. Sometimes an implementing party will share at these meetings a belief that the Tactics are not realistically achievable. If the Responsible Party agrees that this is the case, the Tactics need to be eliminated or changed.

Action Plan Update Meetings Can Motivate Or Demotivate

Seeing measurable progress in accomplishing an Action Plan keeps those working on it committed to accomplishing the Action Plans. If measurable progress is not taking place, employees assigned to carry out the Tactics will not stay motivated when working on Action Plans.

Overcome Reluctance To Expressing Ideas

Sometimes a Responsible Party may come across employees who are reluctant to express their ideas about the Action Plans or Tactics in which they are involved. When this happens, the Responsible Party needs to try to find out why.

Some may have been shut down in the past. You should be able to overcome this if you inform the employees in the Action Plan Update meetings that their feedback matters to you, and call on each employee at the meetings more than once to try to pull out all their feedback and ideas.

Some may have experienced what they believe was retaliation for views they previously expressed. You can overcome this problem if you inform the employees in the Action Plan Update Meetings that you give them your personal assurance that they do not have to worry about any retaliation from you for ideas they express.

Some simply don't believe that anything will be done about any of their ideas, so why waste their time expressing their views. You can overcome this problem if you inform the employees in the Action Plan Update Meetings that their feedback matters to you and that you will try to quickly get back to them on whether the ideas will be implemented. You then need to show them with actions, not just words, how you value their sharing of ideas.

If you are going to use the ideas, be quick to bring about the changes. If the suggestions or ideas from an employee are not going to be implemented, you need to meet with the employee to explain, followed up with an email thanking them for giving the recommendation and explaining why the organization didn't use it.

In some cases, the ideas for changes to the Action Plans may have been good, but the timing for doing it immediately might be wrong. You might want to respond that "We are going to continue with what we are doing, but if we can't get results, your suggested changes will be made. Give a timeline such as: "We need to continue with the present Tactics for several months in order to see if they garner the desired results."

Do Not Permit the Moving of Time Targets

It is essential that the Responsible Party does not permit a culture among those working on an Action Plan in which missing deadlines for specific Tactics is acceptable. It will become a joke among employees if they know they can give a completion date and then, when the date is missed, say without repercussion that, "It wasn't done, but I'll do it by," then giving a new completion date. You may feel it is ok to slip a committed date for a small tactic here and there, but this establishes the culture in your group that deadlines are not important. It is important that you establish a culture from the outset that any and all committed dates must be met. If dates are missed, and some will be, make sure you have the "hard conversations" and that they take the missed deadline seriously.

Protocols and Processes

Successfully achieving Action Plans often requires the Responsible Party to create, or have created and documented, protocols, processes and manuals to provide controls and efficiencies that increase the likelihood of overcoming challenges and/or problems that the Action Plans face. These protocols, processes and manuals may help others working on the Action Plan from having to develop their own protocols, processes and manuals from scratch.

Report Results Of Action Plan Update Meetings To SLT

A Responsible Party should be prepared to summarize the results of their Action Plan Update Meetings when they give his or her update on the Action Plan at the Organization Plan Monitoring Meeting.

SECTION 8

Execution Role of Responsible KDM

Even though this section is devoted to the strategic planning role of the KDM, I strongly recommend all SLT members read this section. The information in this section will help you help your KDM be more effective in leading your organization to success.

I have created a separate section devoted to the execution role of the KDM because your organization can have the best plans in the world, but they'll go nowhere unless your KDM requires disciplined follow through with the execution of the plans. It is, unfortunately, common for KDMs to commit the time needed to create Organization Plans but not be as committed to what is needed to achieving the desired success of the plans.

Every organization I have witnessed who has had poor results from strategic planning has had in common a KDM who did not commit, as needed, to the execution process. In many of the organizations, their KDMs were committed during the important pre-planning-stage and when creating their Organization Plans.

Organizations with the greatest amount of strategic planning success have in common a KDM committed to what is needed to bring about results from their Organization Plans. These KDMs had the discipline to stay focused on each Organization Plan until the Plan Goal was achieved.

KDMs of high-achieving organizations typically share the following Execution Commitment Characteristics, which are covered in this section:

- Allocates Needed Personal Time For Executing Organization Plans
- Requires Action Plan Execution Rather Than Excuses
- Realistic Assignment of Responsibility to Responsible Party
- Effectively Facilitates SLT Meetings
- Knows When It Is Time To "Fold"
- Requires SLT Support on Final Decisions

CHAPTER 22

KDM Allocates Needed Personal Time for Executing Organization Plans

Once an Organization Plan is in place, getting full support from all SLT members is often the difference between the success and failure. The KDM is the one responsible for making sure that every SLT member keeps the organization-wide Plans at the forefront of their day-to-day thinking, so they don't ever lose track of it. If the KDM does not keep it at the forefront of their mind, it won't happen with the SLT.

The most common reason for an organization's strategic planning failure is the lack of focused time commitment by the KDM to strategic planning execution. No matter how good your plans are, it takes leadership and disciplined follow through from your KDM to achieve the Goals of the plans. Without a KDM strategic leadership commitment, an Organization Plan is not likely to succeed, even if it is the best possible plan.

Unless your KDM is totally committed to executing your Organization Plans, your SLT members will be unlikely to have an

> *Your KDM needs to be deeply emotionally involved in driving the implementation of your Organization Plans in order to bring about the needed impact on the organization.*

ongoing high level of commitment for executing the Plans. Generally speaking, without the full demonstrated time commitment of the KDM, an organization's SLT will not maintain the needed Execution Commitment for Organization Plans to succeed, even if the SLT starts out excited about a particular Plan.

A KDM demonstrates a strong commitment to Organization Plan execution by focusing on strategic and longer-term activities that are involved in the plans. This typically requires the KDM to shift some of their focus away from day-to-day fires, while still attending to their essential non-strategic organizational involvement.

Rescheduling Or Cancelling Regularly Scheduled Monthly SLT Meetings

Holding rather than rescheduling or cancelling Organization Plan Monitoring Meetings is essential to succeeding with your Organization Plans. One of the clearest signs of **lack** of KDM time commitment to plan execution is when a KDM has a pattern of frequently cancelling or rescheduling Organization Plan Monitoring Meeting or SLT Annual Retreat Meetings.

This pattern of frequently cancelling or rescheduling these meetings sends a clear message to the SLT that he or she does not view strategic planning as important. The result is that many SLT members will follow the KDM's lead relating to lack of commitment to the organization's strategic planning.

To achieve high-impact strategic planning results for an organization, it is essential the KDM maintain discipline in holding and attending SLT meetings for monitoring actual plan results versus projected results.

Keeping scheduled Organization Plan Monitoring Meetings requires a high level of commitment, self-discipline and self-accountability on the part of the KDM. Regardless of how busy the KDM feels he or she is, these regularly scheduled Organization Plan reviews must not be cancelled unless there is an emergency. They should be treated as if they are set in stone, as it is too easy for things to come up and for meetings to be put off.

Balancing Strategic Planning Execution Against KDM's Day-To-Day Involvement

High-achieving organizations typically have KDMs who accept and embrace the need to allocate time for executing Organization Plans. Execution of the plans is a high priority in their minds, and they balance it against their day-to-day type responsibilities.

It's not always easy for a KDM to focus on implementing strategic plans when inevitably challenged with balancing it against his/her day-to-day tactical or hands-on involvement. However, a KDM needs to keep in mind that for a KDM, there will *always* be something.

The smaller your organization, the more likely a KDM is to be consumed with the detailed, day-to-day aspects of running the organization. It is OK if a KDM has a deep hands-on involvement in certain areas. However, to achieve high impact, the KDM must discipline him or herself to step back from the day-to-day, at times, and invest time in the strategic planning execution that will have the greater long-term impact on the organization.

It's A Marathon Not A Sprint

Many KDMs are more emotionally fit for a sprint than a marathon. They have great passion and excitement for change and have the needed focus to get Organization Plans created. But because of their nature, it is hard for them to keep ongoing focus on making sure their Organization Plans succeed.

One KDM, Paul, has a pattern of losing focus on his Organization Plans before his Organization Goals were reached. He gets very excited about new Organization Plans, but then fails to stay on top of them.

He frequently cancels or reschedules Organization Plan Monitoring Meetings, explaining to his team that he does not have time to attend the meetings.

Understandably, his SLT members were frustrated about the meetings being cancelled or rescheduled, and one of them expressed the SLT's frustration to Paul. Paul worked out an understanding with his Executive Assistant in which she would keep him focused on handling his schedule in such a way that he would attend the meetings. His Executive Assistant also had to give him daily and weekly reminders to adjust his personal schedule to make this happen. Paul stopped rescheduling and cancelling the meetings and execution results for the plans improved in large part because he was staying on top of monitoring results.

The "75 Percent Rule"

I believe an organization will achieve much greater results with strategic planning if the KDM allocates a minimum of 75 percent of his or her work time focused on activities involving the various strategic planning activities that you have read about in this book. These are the "Big Picture Potential" activities that have a high impact on the organization.

One KDM explained to me that the reason he hadn't paid as much attention to the execution of his Organization Plan, as he admitted he should have been doing, was because he was too busy with his other CEO responsibilities. We looked at how he had been spending his time on recurring activities during the previous month. This review identified many things he did which he could delegate to one of his 25 employees. A month after he delegated many of the things he was doing, he said, "I'm amazed at how many of the day-to-day tasks I thought only I could take care of are being done well by my employees."

Reallocating his day-to-day commitments gave him the time to focus on the big picture execution of strategic plans that grow a company. His redistribution of his time to "Big Picture" projects generated increased growth and profit. Also, he received more satisfaction from his work.

CHAPTER 23

KDM Requires Action Plan Execution Rather Than Excuses

Achieving Organization Plan success is dependent on the success of the Action Plans. A common Execution Commitment Characteristic of high-impact KDMs is that they are clear and consistent about requiring Action Plan execution rather than excuses.

A KDM's effective management of deadline accountability of those responsible for Action Plan execution is essential for Organization Plan success. One of the keys to strategically leading an organization is that a KDM not permit Action Plan deadlines to be pushed back repeatedly, because they are so vital to the success of Strategic Plans.

In underperforming companies, it is common for SLT members to believe there will be no ramifications if Action Plan commitments are not met. SLTs in these companies know that the dates are not "real" in the mind of the KDM.

There are different KDM philosophies as to what level of "perfection" the KDM expects for something to be completed on time. When deadline commitments are made in some companies, it is clear to all

SLT members that the KDM expects the work be done as completely or perfectly as can be done. In other companies, there is the KDM philosophy of "done is better than perfect." The key factor here is that the SLT members all understand what the KDM's philosophy is relating to an Action Plan being done.

Identifying Pattern Of Repeatedly Failing To Execute Their Action Plans

A high impact KDM should try to identify, as early as possible, any Responsible Parties for Action Plans who display a pattern of repeatedly failing to execute their Action Plans as committed or completing them only after missing deadlines. It's not hard to identify an employee who has a clear pattern of missing deadlines if the Action Plans are being monitored at the Organization Plan Monitoring Meeting.

Repercussions From KDM Inaction

Before taking any action to address the situation, the KDM needs to identify why the pattern exists. Some Responsible Parties have a pattern of missing commitments because they believe that, based upon past inaction from the KDM, the KDM does not care about them missing deadlines. These parties do not give the needed focus to their commitment because they believe that if they don't achieve it, there are no repercussions.

This attitude of it being acceptable to make a habit of not executing their Action Plans on time is common when a KDM hasn't, in the past, addressed the situation of a Responsible Party who habitually misses deadlines. When you think about it, why should a Responsible Party take the commitments seriously or believe not keeping commitments will affect their careers when a KDM demonstrates that he or she does not take any action when commitments are not met.

> *If Responsible Parties for the results of Action Plans believe missing time commitments for achieving results is acceptable, many commitments will be missed.*

Whenever an Action Plan deadline is missed and there are no repercussions, it reinforces an attitude within the SLT of, "Well, if *that person* can miss a deadline and no one cares, why should I care about meeting *my* deadlines?" This attitude builds roadblocks for the Organization Plan as a whole ... and eventually keeps the Organization Plan from achieving its Goal.

Actions Give A Clear Message That Action Plan Commitments Must Be Met

A missed date is bound to happen, but it cannot become the norm. Habitual missing of Action Plan deadlines by Responsible Parties is not tolerated by high-impact KDMs. The need to keep Action Plan commitments will not be clearly understood by SLT members without action by the KDM when commitments are missed. If a pattern of missed commitments is not addressed, the organization will have a never-ending problem with some SLT members failing to keep execution commitments.

> *A KDM should not sit back and do nothing when the Action Plans aren't being completed to his or her satisfaction.*

KDMs should explain in person to their SLT that Action Plan completion dates do matter to them and are set in stone unless there is a legitimate excuse that has been communicated to all involved parties **well before the committed-to completion date. But talk by KDMs is not enough if actions are not consistent with the verbal message.**

Getting Control Back

If a KDM has been letting missed commitments slide, how does the KDM change the situation? A KDM needs to find out the "why" before deciding how to correct the problem of missed Action Plan deadlines. Then action needs to happen.

Let's look at how one KDM changed things. He had allowed his operations manager, who was the Responsible Party for several Action

Plans, to continuously miss commitment dates with no repercussions. This established a culture where other SLT members did not feel an urgency to meet their dates either. This SLT culture was responsible for the lack of progress towards the organization's Goal.

To get things back on track, the KDM opened an Organization Plan Monitoring Meeting with a statement that "missed commitment dates would no longer be permitted". He explained that, going forward, the Responsible Party for any Action Plan should think long and hard before agreeing to completion dates and should let the SLT know well in advance if making a date was in jeopardy. He added that once those dates were set, he expected them to be met unless the SLT was informed well in advance that there was a problem, and the problem turned out to be legitimate. He suggested it would be good practice for Responsible Parties to complete their commitments ahead of the schedule rather than behind it, so as to play it safe.

> *Action, not just talk, is needed when results are not delivered by committed-to timelines. If there are repercussions, future committed results are more likely to happen.*

After this policy was put in place by the KDM, his operations manager missed two committed dates. The KDM wrote up a formal letter to go into the personnel file for the operations manager. The KDM met with the operations manager to go over a copy of the write-up and discuss it. This upset the operations manager who mentioned it to the other SLT managers. Interestingly, after the one write-up, all his managers began to give realistic deadlines that could be met and began making most of them. The implementation of repercussions for lack of proper follow-through was the crucial factor in getting all SLT members to take deadlines seriously.

KDMs With Confrontation Problems

For some KDMs, it is uncomfortable for them to enforce Responsible Party accountability. If a KDM has a problem taking the actions needed, the KDM must determine a way that will work for him or her.

One KDM, who is an excellent "people person," was not doing what he needed to do to make his Organization Plans succeed, because he goes out of his way to avoid conflicts. The KDM's conflict avoidance resulted in him not taking the necessary tough actions with a member of the SLT who, as a Responsible Party for Action Plans, consistently missed the Action Plan commitments. KDMs must hold all SLT members to the same standards of execution. It is demoralizing to a SLT if a KDM shows even the appearance of a protected SLT member by giving any special treatment at SLT meetings, such as holding one of the SLT members to a different level of expectations.

So it should be no surprise that the other SLT members were not happy about the situation. A couple of the other SLT members brought up to the KDM their concern with the lack of required accountability when the other member did not deliver on the Action Plans. They pointed out to the KDM how he did not address the issues and did not set any consequences.

What they said was true, and it was because the KDM dreaded face-to-face conflict. So the KDM sent an email to all his SLT members explaining that if any of them missed committed deadlines, as a pattern, they would be removed from the SLT and could be out of a job. It was interesting that shortly after the email was sent, committed results for Action Plans started to take place in a consistent manner by the same SLT member who had not kept his commitments in the past.

CHAPTER 24

KDM Realistic Assignment of Responsibility to Responsible Party

When projected Action Plan results are not taking place within the committed-to timelines, you may hear a variety of excuses from Responsible Parties. The challenge is to find the real "why."

The "why" may be that the Responsible Party is not capable of being the Responsible Party. The party might lack tenacity and ability to manage personal time to execute the Action Plan.

Sometimes the problem is that a Responsible Party does not have the ability to push back against unrealistically attainable Action Plan dates.

Sometimes getting results means the KDM will have to replace unproductive Responsible Parties. For example, the "why" may be that an Action Plan requires competency that the Responsible Party does not have. If this happens, it is important to give the responsibility for an Action Plan to another SLT member with the correct capabilities, rather than assuming that an Action Plan cannot succeed.

When an Action Plan is not hitting its mark, the KDM needs to perform an objective evaluation of whether the SLT member has the right talent and commitment to be the Responsible Party for the execution of Action Plans. Some people are capable of helping to develop good plans but are not of much value in doing what is needed to get results from the plans. Some are great at carrying out their own project plans but are not effective at managing others to perform the tasks needed for Action Plans to get results.

KDMs who run high-impact organizations make sure the right people are designated as Responsible Parties for Action Plans. If they don't select the right people at first, they replace them with those who are best suited for the job. Some KDMs have a tendency to overlook or rationalize the deficiencies of some SLT members and give them Responsible Party duties because of an emotional attachment to the person or because they have invested time in that person.

If the problem is that a SLT member doesn't have 'the right stuff', whether it is ability or attitude, the KDM is the only one who has the authority to do something about it. The KDM must act, even if it means taking a step backwards temporarily while a new Responsible Party gets "up to speed" on an Action Plan. I believe it is sometimes better to cut your losses as soon as possible rather than hold onto someone as the Responsible Party who is not going to move the Action Plan forward in the required way.

Carol determined that her Organization Plan, which had an Action Plan focused on certain sales results, was not going to succeed, as her sales manager, who was a great salesperson, was the wrong one to be the Responsible Party for the very important Action Plan. She therefore reassigned it to her EVP. It was difficult to let the sales manager know the EVP of the company would be taking over as the Responsible Party for the Action Plan, because she really liked him as a person; he simply was not the right person for the job. Within a few months, the new Responsible Party was getting better results, and her sales manager continued to excel at what he had always been good at — selling.

There will be times the KDM has to go deeper into understanding the obstacles to some of the Tactics of an Action Plan to understand why the Action Plan is not meeting expectations. The KDM should discuss with the Responsible Party how to overcome these obstacles, without excuses, in a timely manner, to ensure your Action Plan succeeds. Sometimes this requires changes and modifications.

The KDM must recognize that a Responsible Party cannot do everything all at the same time. The KDM must determine whether being responsible for a particular Action Plan should be the priority of the person. This type of thinking may require the KDM to eliminate or greatly change the timeline of assigned Action Plans. An example of how this was done poorly by a KDM involved a technology company that had an Organization Plan with a Goal of acquiring a specific number of new clients. The Director of Marketing was the Responsible Party for several of the Action Plans.

One KDM's motto for Action Plan updates at Organization Plan Monitoring Meetings is understood by all SLT members when giving their updates: "No excuses, just the facts."

The Director of Marketing, however, was torn between what he saw as the needs for his time to be spent, in a very hands-on capacity, on these Action Plans and the act of managing his department. He didn't speak up about this concern and didn't put in place the things needed for the Action Plans to succeed.

When the Responsible Party explained at a monthly meeting that he had not achieved projected results for the Action Plans, he also acknowledged that he failed because he did not have the necessary time to get the Action Plans accomplished. Things should never get to this point if, in setting expectations of a Responsible Party, they understand the importance of realistic deadlines and advanced communication about missing deadlines.

CHAPTER 25

KDM Effectively Facilitates SLT Meetings

The KDM, or an outside party appointed by the KDM, are the only ones who should facilitate the SLT meetings. There may be instances when the KDM, or a designated outside facilitator, is not available, but these situations should be rare rather than frequent. In these instances, it is allowable for facilitation to be delegated to another SLT member. Consequently, I will be referring to the person providing the facilitation activity as the Facilitator, whether or not the person is the KDM.

Facilitating Organization Plan Monitoring Meetings should follow a two-step protocol that starts with reviewing and then addressing, as needed, each of your Organization Plans, one plan at a time. The driving Organization Plan should be the first plan the facilitator brings up for review. The second step is to facilitate bringing out ideas from all SLT members for adjustments to both Strategies and Action Plans. SLT members need to be open to suggestions for Strategy and Action Plan adjustments, regardless of what member first came up with the Strategies or Action Plans. Discussing adjustments is sometimes very difficult for team members whose natural behavior style is to be uncomfortable with change.

Each Responsible Party for Action Plans that are part of an Organization Plan you are reviewing needs to be allocated sufficient time to present an update at the SLT meetings of the Action Plan for which he or she is responsible. The amount of time needed for the reports differ with the complexity of the plan and challenges that may be occurring. Your SLT members typically will have questions for the Responsible Party. The report, including the questions and answers relating to the report, needs to be complete before discussions are opened up that may include suggestions for changes.

The following are the types of questions a KDM should ask a Responsible Party at SLT Meetings when reviewing the status of Action Plan commitments:

- What are the measured results of the Action Plan compared to projected results?
- Are the projected results on track? (Yes or No)
- If the projected results of the Action Plan are not on track, ask what caused the poor results. These reasons need to be understood before the SLT should try to overcome the roadblocks that stand in the way of success.
- Are all Tactics or just some of the Tactics not being completed on schedule?
- If the Action Plan is not on track, what does the Responsible Party feel is needed to get on track?
- If the Responsible Party feels the Action Plan can't get back on track, what is the suggestion, if any, for a new track for the Action Plan?

There may be times when the Facilitator needs feedback and expertise of employees who are not SLT members but who are performing tasks relating to Action Plans. They may be needed to update status information or report on projected progress, or lack thereof. The Facilitator will call these employees into your SLT meetings for specific discussions that require their input.

When the reporting Responsible Party makes his or her update presentation to discuss the actual versus projected results, you should expect different viewpoints from other SLT members. But viewpoints should not be expressed in a way that is emotional or confrontational. When disrespect is displayed, it is important the Facilitator reinforce respect for each other's views.

At the end of the meeting, the Facilitator should point out what the Facilitator sees as the priorities for the next monthly meeting, to help the team maintain focus in between meetings.

Being a good SLT meeting Facilitator also includes the need for the KDM, whether or not the KDM is the Facilitator, to personally be "Open To The Views Of Others". This mind-set is needed to make the adjustments that will bring about success of the Plans. Your KDM must be open to views of the other SLT members or results of the Organization Plans will suffer.

Let me share with you an example where the openness was not present. When one KDM started her SLT meetings, she was charming and personable. However, whenever one of her managers challenged her views about staying the course with Action Plans rather than making suggested changes, the KDM switched from a charming business owner to one who blew up and defended her position by yelling.

How do you think that KDM's loud outburst affected the atmosphere for the rest of the team? She had a pattern of raising her voice in meetings when responding to suggestions with which she disagreed. What do you think were the chances she received total openness from her SLT on views that differed from hers? Not surprisingly, the other SLT members did not challenge or offer feedback on anything they thought the KDM might see as being against her views.

After being told by her one day that she questioned the value of meeting monthly with her SLT to discuss the execution results of their Organization Plans, I asked her if she would invite me to sit in on one of the SLT meetings. Her lack of openness to her SLT's ideas was quickly apparent. When we had lunch following the meeting, I told the KDM how she stifled feedback from those team members who disagreed with her views. She responded, only half jokingly, that she was totally behind getting ideas from others at the meetings, but with this caveat: "As long as my employees understand that in my company, the only ideas that count are those of the owner, the owner and the owner."

I explained to her that to get the most effective results from Organization Plans, she needed to create an atmosphere at SLT meetings where her employees felt they could be open with her. After a lot of discussion, she agreed to listen openly to challenges to her perspective at the company's next Organization Plan Monitoring Meeting and to try hard to control her tendency to attack any views that differed with hers.

Sometime later, the KDM acknowledged to me that, "I'm glad I allowed my managers to challenge my thinking, because it has resulted in so many positive changes to our Plans that I did not like initially."

> *If your SLT members challenge your KDM's ideas or have questions about a change they want to explore, it's important they always feel free to share their thoughts with their KDM.*

Only extreme situations should excuse a KDM from attending the great majority of Organization Plan Monitoring Meetings. One extreme example involved a heart attack by one KDM. During the time the KDM was not able to attend the meetings for health reasons, he appointed one of the SLT members to take over his SLT meeting facilitating responsibilities. As part of this solution, the KDM started holding monthly meetings with the SLT member who had temporarily taken over the facilitation role so that the KDM could keep abreast of things relating to the Organization Plan.

One SLT member of an organization told me about the team's frustration that their monthly four-hour SLT meeting to review three Organization Plans never progressed more than halfway through monitoring the first plan. He explained that the KDM wanted a report on every Tactic in every Action Plan. Going through the status of enormous amounts of Tactics took up so much of the meeting time that he felt the meeting was a waste of time.

CHAPTER 26

KDM Knows When It Is Time to "Fold"

A high-impact KDM recognizes when revisions are needed and shows the leadership force for making timely revisions to Organization Action Plans when required. But sometimes this isn't enough to result in the Plans succeeding.

Often the SLT member who initially sponsored the Organization Plan pushes to keep it in existence long after it should have been removed. This member may see the need to continue with the Plan because of fear that eliminating the Plan would seem to be the personal failure of the party who originally pushed for that Plan. This SLT member often uses a rationalization such as, "so much money has already been invested in the Plan that we need to see it succeed."

Other SLT members may not want to enter into the fight that would result from questioning whether it is time to give up on the Plan. As a result, the Organization Plan stays on too long and is treated as sacrosanct, even after it is clear the problems with the Plan are very hard to fix, remove or change. The Plan is treated by the SLT as not allowed to be touched or challenged, no matter how damaging its continued existence may be for the organization.

High-impact KDMs do not continue funding Organization Plans just because the idea was a good one when the Plan was first created. At one technology company, there was an Organization Plan to create a software package for another company. The Director of IT originally budgeted $500,000 to get the finished software package ready to be sold. But, after it not being ready on time, the KDM had become dissatisfied with the quality control of the software development, which was delaying the product. He worked with the Director of IT on ways to improve the quality control so the software product could be rolled out.

After another two years, the KDM brought up at a SLT meeting that the software product was still not working properly. He pointed out that considering all costs, including the payments to outside resources and the real cost of company personnel time spent on the project, over $3,000,000 had been sunk into creating the software. The Director of IT explained that the product was almost ready, as he had stated at many previous Organization Plan Monitoring Meetings.

The KDM eliminated that Organization Plan, explaining, "It's time we cut our losses." A couple of other SLT members, after the meeting, privately told the KDM they were glad the Organization Plan was dropped. Interestingly, neither had spoken up against the Director of IT during the Organization Plan Monitoring Meeting with any views of dropping the plan.

The good news is that the resources were reallocated to allow the funding of another Organization Plan that did bring about positive bottom line results for the company.

Sometimes the KDM needs to eliminate or "fold" an Organization Plan in order to not allow too much on the organization planning "plate."

CHAPTER 27

KDM Requires SLT Support
on Final Decisions

My last area of discussion concerning the KDM's execution commitment role involves making sure there is aligned support from the SLT for each finalized Organization Plan, as well as all other top-level KDM finalized decisions. A KDM should be able to expect full support of the decision from all SLT members, whether or not they agreed with the decision. Once the decision is made, it's essential they totally support making the decision succeed or they should not be reporting to the KDM.

From the time I first found myself in a leadership position, I have tried to make it clear to those reporting to me that they can disagree with me and share the reasons why they disagree with me. But they must support my final decisions. My SLT members know they are welcome to question or challenge any of my decisions directly, face to face, and that I will listen to their thinking and discuss my reasoning on things. When this isn't the case, getting success from strategic planning can be problematical.

One SLT had a lot of discussions about an Organization Plan that included a strategy for changing the way the company priced its products. For decades, the manufacturing company had sold its products by negotiating the price. However, the KDM thought it might be a good idea to stick to prices that were non-negotiable. She explained her view that eliminating negotiated pricing would benefit the company because customers would feel more confident that they were getting the right price the first time. She added that it would require a period of adjustment for those used to negotiating, but the change would ultimately result in increased sales and profits.

The KDM discussed her ideas about the new product-pricing model with her SLT and encouraged them to express their views on the Organization DCSF Plan. Her sales manager expressed his fear that company sales would be hurt. After further discussions with the SLT, they decided to create a plan that had a Goal of creating the non-negotiable pricing model the KDM wanted.

A week after the meeting, the KDM found out her sales manager was telling other employees he thought the new Plan would "destroy" the company. The KDM met with the sales manager and explained that his comments of concern were not acceptable after the decision was made to move ahead with the Organization Plan. She also explained that if he could not support the Organization Plan for revising the pricing model, he should not be part of the organization. As it turned out, the plan for changing the pricing model was a great success.

One of the common challenges to KDMs is the resistance of some SLT members to change. Those who fight putting certain things into Plans because they are against change will only support it in a "lukewarm" or even passive aggressive manner.

High-performing organizations that have success in accomplishing their Organization Plans are typically organizations that embrace change. Change and innovation need to be a guiding way of life for Organization Plans to succeed. Innovation is a way of life for highly performing organizations, and it must be conveyed that you are open to innovative ways of accomplishing the Goal.

Your KDM should lead the way in getting your organization to embrace the change needed for achieving Goals. This may require the KDM remove systems and/or processes that time and experience have shown to be ineffective, or test and adapt new approaches. It may require the KDM taking strong positions with employees, at any level, who do not embrace required change.

Some parts of our workplace culture are more likely to support organizational progress than others. Inevitably, I have found employee groups that do not embrace change reporting to SLT members are themselves against the change represented by a Plan. The KDM is the only one who has the authority to insure that needed SLT member support is happening.

CONCLUSION

You now have the tools and techniques for strategically leading your organization to achieve the desired long-term Organization Vision. Using StratPro in your organization will bring about more than a higher level of success. It will make the work-related time spent by your SLT members, including your KDM, more enjoyable with less work-related stress.

One year after her company started using StratPro, one KDM explained to me that her company was achieving more and she was now enjoying her work time versus often dreading it. She stated: "Within months of when we started to implement our first Organization Plan, I saw a difference. Before, I had a lot of good ideas, but I wasn't running the business strategically. Identifying and working on our first two written Organization Plans created positive energy with strategic direction for our company."

Once started, the pre-planning, planning and execution commitment for your organization's StratPro strategic planning will be ongoing. The key is to get started with StratPro NOW!

Although this book was written so your organization could

undertake StratPro strategic planning without a specialist, there are certified StratPro Implementers available to help your organization with every step of the StratPro strategic planning process, both through workshops and hands-on involvement.

However, some KDMs simply do not feel comfortable facilitating meetings and driving plans. It's ok if you feel you don't have all the traits necessary to drive StratPro with the focus needed. If you feel it would help your organization's StratPro involvement, a Certified StratPro Implementer can help your SLT with every step of the StratPro process, including running workshops for your SLTs and facilitating your SLT meetings. Our professionals will help ensure the necessary SLT meetings take place and that there is a team-meeting environment so that none of the team members will be hesitant to share their views, even if they disagree with each other. Sometimes KDMs have trouble bringing about this openness.

Your StratPro Implementer can bring your organization the structure needed to ensure that scheduled meetings take place and have the facilitation skills to get the most out of the meetings.

You may have a world of information concerning your organization in your head, but sometimes seeing things from the perspective of others, who are not in your organization or even your industry, will challenge your thinking in a way that significantly improves your organization's strategic planning results.

There are also delicate matters for which a KDM can benefit from a StratPro Implementer. The most effective way to get objective answers by SLT members to the Diagnostic Questionnaire and the views about the organization SWOT is with an outside specialist who meets individually with the team members and the KDM. In most cases, the information of how each SLT member answers the diagnostic and the SWOT is shared only with the KDM or individuals selected by the KDM.

Another example is when a business owner may desire bringing a son or daughter into the organization. However, for whatever reason, the business owner does not want this information expressed during meetings dealing with the creation of the company's formal strategic plans. A StratPro Implementer may be able to help with the integration of the son/daughter into the organization. They may make the transition easier on him/her and for your non-family member employees.

I wish you all the very best in achieving the vision of your organization and creating a greater balance in your life.

Allen Fishman

CPSIA information can be obtained
at www.ICGtesting.com
Printed in the USA
FSHW01n1203210918
52200FS